8.95

Functions of E

A course for up

and more advan

CW00524666

Teacher's Book

Leo Jones

Cambridge University Press
Cambridge
New York Port Chester
Melbourne Sydney

Published by the Press Syndicate of the University of Cambridge
The Pitt Building, Trumpington Street, Cambridge CB2 1RP
40 West 20th Street, New York, NY 10011, USA
10 Stamford Road, Oakleigh, Melbourne 3166, Australia

© Cambridge University Press 1981

First published 1981
Fourth printing1990

Printed in Great Britain at the
University Press, Cambridge

ISBN 0 521 28248 9 Teacher's Book
ISBN 0 521 28249 7 Student's Book
ISBN 0 521 23836 6 Cassette

Recorded Exercises
ISBN 0 521 28382 5 Student's Workbook
ISBN 0 521 26353 0 Set of 3 cassettes

Copyright
The law allows a reader to make a single copy of part of a book for purposes of private study. It does not allow the copying of entire books or the making of multiple copies of extracts. Written permission for any such copying must always be obtained from the publisher in advance.

WP

Contents

Acknowledgements

Thanks again to the following friends and colleagues who gave me so much advice and encouragement in the development of the first edition of this book: John Forster, Sue Gosling, Diana Maddock, Michael Roberts, Rob Shave, Ken Tooke, Karen and Peter Viney, Katy Walker, Sally and Guy Wellman.

Many thanks to all my colleagues, old and new, who helped me to test this second edition so thoroughly, spotted the things which were not quite right and suggested numerous improvements. And thanks to all the students from all over the world who used it and made their comments. And a big thank you to Kay McKechnie for guiding the book so efficiently and understandingly through its final stages. Finally, many, many thanks to C. von Baeyer, whose painstaking and imaginative work on the forthcoming North American edition has contributed so many improvements to this British edition.

Acknowledgements

Introduction

Functions of English is a book for upper-intermediate and more advanced students, and it is organized on *functional* lines. This introduction describes some of the advantages of the functional approach, as well as the way in which the functional material in the book is organized.

Who needs *Functions of English*?

Most upper-intermediate and advanced students have spent a lot of time learning basic English grammar and have a good knowledge of everyday English vocabulary. But time and again, students have found that a knowledge of grammar and vocabulary is not enough to be an effective speaker of English in the real world outside the classroom. It is also essential to learn how to *do* things with language – how to use words and structures to do the things we want to do, whether it is to persuade a friend to do something, to describe a machine to a group of people, or whatever.

For students to acquire this *communicative competence* they must learn more than just grammar and vocabulary. They must learn which structures are *appropriate* to the situation they are in and the people they are with. They must learn to use a range of expressions (some of which they already know, some of which are new) that are commonly used to agree, to complain, to discuss the future, and so on. They must learn to conduct conversations – beginnings, middles, and endings – which are fluent and natural.

The functional approach provides a means of organizing all the material which must be mastered before a person can be said to have 'learned a language'. The approach involves isolating certain *language functions*, such as 'asking for information' (unit 2), 'refusing to do something' (unit 3), 'giving an opinion' (unit 8), etc. These functions are then learnt by practising them in a variety of everyday situations. Each situation involves people in useful *roles* (friend, stranger, employee, customer), with typical *settings* (on a plane, at a party, at a meeting), and with likely *topics* (business, travel, sport).

The emphasis is on developing *fluency* – giving students lots of practice in dealing with frequently-encountered functions and situations. Any student who ever intends to *use* the languag can benefit.

What good is the functional approach?

The functional approach does not *replace* traditional language teaching – it adds a new dimension to it. Grammar and vocabulary still have to be learnt – for example, students must know how to use future verb forms before they can talk about the future in real-life situations involving making predictions and stating intentions (as in unit 6).

Some revision may be necessary before the material is tackled. *Notions in English* (CUP 1979) is designed to be used for this kind of work (and units 10, 11 and 19 in *Notions in English* are useful preparation for unit 6 in *Functions of English*). The two books can be used in parallel to provide a course which covers not only functions, but also grammar and vocabulary by dealing with specific notions (topics) and general notions (concepts expressed through grammar and vocabulary). There is no unit-to-unit relationship between the two books, however, so they can be used independently.

Work on a unit in this book may bring to light a need for revision or extra work on particular areas of grammar or vocabulary afterwards, too. Careful monitoring of your students' performance and taking account of the questions they ask will help you to pinpoint such areas. Remember, though, that grammar and vocabulary are simply tools needed to communicate naturally in speaking and in writing. The goal is clearly communication – first in class and then outside it.

The aim of the functional approach is to get students in class to engage in communication that is as close as possible to the 'real thing'. This aim is achieved by special emphasis on two principles:

– Students must be involved in as many situations as possible where one of them has some information and another one doesn't but has to get it. Such situations are said to contain an *information gap* between the participants – in the usual classroom situation the student is often being told information he or she already knows and this is not realistic. The communication activities described below have been specially designed to create such information gaps.
– Students must be involved in as many situations as possible where they must *choose* from a variety of expressions. Several

different ways of putting a function into words must be learnt – there is never just one way of achieving an aim with language. Students may settle on favourite expressions, but they must also understand many different ways of expressing any function. The lists of language items in the presentation sections in every unit (see below) provide many opportunities for the students to make choices.

What does the teacher do in *Functions of English*?

This book encourages a very active approach to language practice. There are many different types of exercises and activities that stimulate a lot of talking and will often be amusing. These will increase the confidence of students and improve their accuracy in conversation. Students are often asked to play different roles – and it is only fair that you the teacher should sometimes join in. Playing a role does not demand any acting skill or funny clothes and voices – it just requires careful scene-setting and some 'willing suspension of disbelief'.

As with any textbook, you will find that there are things you want to leave out and things you want to put in – any adaptation of the material to suit the needs and interests of your class will make the book more functional! The questionnaire in unit 1 is a good starting point for finding out from your class what their needs, interests and expectations really are.

Functions of English will help improve students' listening, speaking and writing skills, but your class may need further work in reading and also supplementary listening practice. Such extra material is best chosen personally by the teacher to suit the needs and interests of the class.

How is the *new edition* different from the *first edition*?

The first edition of *Functions of English* has been used with great success since 1977 in many different teaching situations. Comments from teachers and students made it clear that there was room for improvement and that a rewritten version would achieve its aims much better. This revised edition is intended to make the book easier for teachers to use, more exciting for students and above all more *communicative*.

The main changes and additions are:

1 *Conversations*: these have all been re-recorded to make them more relevant and more interesting.
2 *Presentation*: these sections have been expanded and, in some

cases, given a different emphasis (see units 6, 8, 10 and 15, for example). They have also been re-recorded.

3 *Practice*: most of these sections have been improved and many of them have been replaced with ideas that work better.
4 *Communication activities*: these are entirely new. The technique used is described on page 10, and helps to make the free practice of each function more communicative and more spontaneous.
5 *Teacher's Book*: this is also entirely new. It is more of a guidebook than an instruction manual. It provides the teacher with plenty of extra ideas and gives an overview of what happens in each section of the Student's Book.
6 *Recorded Exercises*: also entirely new. The tapescript is at the back of the Teacher's Book, where you will also find a full description of the exercises (on page 97). The recorded exercises provide extra practice on each unit and can be used in a language laboratory or by students on their own with a cassette recorder. There is a set of three cassettes and a workbook, which students using the exercises need to have.

How is *Functions of English* organized?

The Student's Book and the Teacher's Book both consist of an introduction and fifteen units (each consisting of between nine and fifteen sections). The Student's Book contains the lesson material and the 153 communication activities. The Teacher's Book contains notes and additional suggestions on every section and also the tapescript of the recorded exercises.

One unit would normally take 3–4 lessons to cover, but preliminary revision and extra time spent on correcting students' mistakes and preparing the written work could expand the time required to 5–6 lessons. Similarly, if a particular unit is of great interest or relevance to a group of students extra time should be spent on it. As a rough guide, one presentation and the two or three practice sections and communication activities which follow it might take about 45–60 minutes to do in class.

Each unit is divided into several sections:

Unit title

The title of each unit states the major functions which are focussed on, usually three of them.

Functional objectives (only in Teacher's Book)

A short statement is given of the abilities that students will focus on in that unit. These objectives should be outlined to your students before the unit is done in terms they can appreciate – by referring to their own jobs, interests and needs, for example. It is also essential to assess the achievement of these objectives while working on a unit and to ask the students if they feel they have achieved them by the end of the unit. A simple question like 'What do you think you've learnt from this unit?' might be a suitable way of finding out.

Presupposed knowledge (only in Teacher's Book)

This section is not included in every unit, but where it is, there is a list of the basic grammatical structures needed to perform the language functions in that unit. If a short assessment of your students' knowledge shows that they cannot use these structures, they will need preliminary revision and practice before starting the unit. Relevant units in *Notions in English* are noted in the Teacher's Book and these are designed to be used as preparatory material for *Functions of English*. Another suitable book is *English in Situations* by Robert O'Neill (OUP 1970) and relevant sections in this are noted in this Teacher's Book. If you do not find it necessary to do such preliminary revision and practice, or if you need to interrupt your students' work on a unit in this book to revise a grammatical point, make sure your students are aware of *why* they are doing this revision.

Conversation

Content Each unit begins with an unscripted conversation. This is *not* a 'dialogue' which students should learn by heart. Its purpose is to demonstrate the functions focussed on in the unit being performed in a typical situation. In this way, students are introduced to some of the exponents of the language functions and can see how they are used by native speakers of English in a real conversation. The transcripts reproduce the conversations as faithfully as possible and include the hesitations and imperfections of spoken English, but they cannot show all the features of stress, intonation, tone of voice and articulation that are heard on the recording.

Procedure A good way to use the conversations on tape is as follows:

1 Play the entire conversation once or twice and then ask general comprehension and summary questions. Discuss the relationship between the speakers.

2 Play the conversation and ask the students to spot examples of the language functions being performed. Get them to mark these in their books. Discuss the effect or 'force' of each example on the listener.

3 Play the conversation, stopping it frequently before a speaker has finished and ask: What's he or she going to say next?' This will help to train students to *predict* or *anticipate* what people are going to say – an essential skill in understanding spoken English.

4 Discuss with the class any ideas or language points arising from the conversation.

Giving more examples The conversations can demonstrate only a few of the exponents of the language functions. You may have to give further examples of your own to demonstrate the use of the other expressions presented later on.

Variety It is a good idea to use a variety of procedures with the conversations: sometimes play it at the *end* of a unit, sometimes concentrate on steps 1 and 2 above, sometimes start with step 3 and sometimes use the alternative ideas suggested in the Teacher's Book.

Teacher's Book In the Teacher's Book there are alternative ideas for introducing each unit. The first three conversations are reproduced in the form of an 'annotated' transcript with the exponents printed in italics and places for pausing the tape indicated for the step 3 prediction or anticipation questions.

Presentation

Content Each presentation section describes the function and lists several exponents. Advice is given on the use of these, where necessary. Each unit has three presentation sections each followed by several practice activities. These presentation sections are recorded on the tape.

Procedure Students should be asked to prepare these sections by reading them through before you cover them in class. A good way to handle the presentation sections is to get the students to close their books and for you to use the tape and the board. The tape presents the language items in a lively way, and you can then provide further information and personal advice on how and when to use them appropriately.

Alternatively, provided your students have all prepared the section beforehand, you can call on them to remember expressions, so that ideas will come from them – it's always better for students to make suggestions than for the teacher to 'spoonfeed' them.

Whichever procedure you use, allow your students to introduce similar expressions from their own experience. Ask them to suggest examples of each expression in use. Make sure they can decide when each expression would be appropriate.

Changing expressions You are encouraged to change the lists of language items that are provided in the presentation sections to suit your own or the local way of speaking. You should feel free to add, drop, or modify items. (If you are not sure about the appropriateness of an item, ask a native speaker about it.) In any case, you may decide to concentrate your teaching on a selection of items that is not too easy nor too hard for your class.

Choice of expressions From the set of language items that you cover in class – there should always be several for each function – your students should be free to choose a few as their own favourites. The focus of each lesson should be on *understanding* functions expressed in a wide variety of ways, but *expressing* functions in a few ways that the students feel most comfortable with. This element of choosing some expressions from a possible range is precisely what fluent speakers of a language do all the time – we know more expressions than we use, and we must always make a quick choice of one expression to use in any given situation.

Unpredictable language Some of the essential information is not given in the presentation section at all – often it is what students say *after* an introductory phrase being presented that is the important thing. But, since no one can predict what a student will actually want to say after 'As I see it . . .', for example, this information cannot be given in the book. Whatever the students say, you must be prepared to correct mistakes, provide some necessary vocabulary or offer advice on usage. True communication, which is the aim at this level of language learning, is basically unpredictable. Although dealing with this sort of unpredictable language may seem very demanding, it is certainly also extremely rewarding and it is an essential part of training students to actually communicate their ideas.

Pronunciation and simple drills

It will usually be necessary for you to do some controlled pronunciation practice – the tape will be useful for this. Students need to be able to feel comfortable pronouncing an expression, especially if it's a long one, before they can start to use it. Pay particular attention to the *tone of voice* your students use – do they sound sufficiently polite, interested, modest etc.? Apart from repetition of the new expressions in short sentences, your students may also benefit from some simple drills on the recommended expressions before they move on to the practice sections. Such drills would normally be improvised, but there are several suggestions in the Teacher's Book.

Teacher's Book

Additional expressions are given in the Teacher's Book, some of which you may want to teach. There are also notes on points to watch and suggestions for simple drills or manipulation practice.

Practice

There are two different kinds of practice sections.

Teacher-controlled practice

The first practice section after each presentation section is usually 'teacher-controlled', so that you have a chance to advise and correct your class before the freer practice sections. Try to concentrate on helping the students to express themselves. Encourage them not to play safe, but to experiment. Help them to concentrate on using the recommended expressions. Encourage them to use some 'new' expressions rather than just the 'easy' expressions they know already. You may need to interrupt frequently during this first practice section.

Freer practice

The later practice sections are much freer. They are designed to build confidence and fluency. Many of these sections require students to work together in pairs or small groups. It is important to set the scene very carefully in many of these practice sections so that the students know exactly what they have to do and can get involved in the situation. Such scene-setting comes to life more if you do it in your own personal way, rather than relying on the printed words in the book.

Procedures: Monitoring mistakes

In the freer practice sections, it is important not to interrupt students in the middle of a sentence or conversation just because a mistake has been made. This does not mean that the teacher can sit back and relax – you should go around the room *monitoring* the conversations. This involves making notes of some good, and some not-so-good, ways of expressing oneself that you hear (these will be used later). Help students who are stuck, but try not to give too much help – otherwise students will come to rely on you for constant help. And don't correct every mistake – otherwise the students may become too mistake-conscious and tongue-tied. You will find the students correcting each other as they get used to this kind of practice and this can be very effective if it is not overdone. Make sure you pause for question time after each practice section, letting the students air their difficulties and giving you a chance to discuss what you heard as you went around the room.

Repeating practice

You may find that the students had so much trouble with a particular practice section that you may want to do it all over again, perhaps in rearranged groups. This kind of 'replay' can increase confidence greatly and provide a tangible feeling of sudden progress, which is often lacking at this level of language learning, and which students often find reassuring.

The odd man out

One minor problem in pair work is that in a class with an odd number of students, one person is left over after the rest of the class have formed into pairs – this is easily solved by putting the extra student to work with another to make a group of three. Suggestions for the handling of an extra student are given wherever necessary in the notes on each unit in the Teacher's Book.

Changing partners

Do not allow students to talk to the same partner every time. Rearrange seating regularly or make sure that students change partners frequently. The reason for this is that students can easily get bored or frustrated with a regular partner; it also makes the practice more interesting by giving students a chance to talk to different people – and it makes the conversations more unpredictable and so more realistic.

Recording and performing

If possible, from time to time, record one of the groups in action on tape (or even on video) and play back the recording for analysis by the rest of the class. And, from time to time, ask a group to 'perform' in front of the class after they have 'rehearsed' their conversation.

Benefits of pair and group work The rationale behind pair or group work may need to be explained to students who feel that they should be constantly corrected by the teacher, or that the teacher should control the whole lesson. Reasons for using pair and group work in this book include the following:

- The amount of student talking time is greatly increased, and the more the students talk, the more fluent they become.
- Students feel less inhibited when talking privately to another student than when they are talking in front of the whole class. When they are less inhibited, they experiment more, and discover how much they can actually communicate with the English they know already.
- Playing roles in the exercises prepares students in a non-threatening way for the roles they may need to play in real-life situations in English.

Teacher's Book Additional teacher-controlled practice ideas are given in the Teacher's Book. There are also ideas for additional free practice.

Communication activities

Content The communication activities provide the freest practice of all. These involve two or more sides communicating with each other in discussions, role-plays, problem-solving activities etc.

Format The communication activity sections in the individual units give instructions on how to divide up the class and at what activity number to begin in the communication activity collection at the back of the Student's Book. One activity at the back of the book often leads to another until the students are instructed to re-assemble as a class, discuss, and proceed with the unit they were studying. (A bookmark may come in handy for students to keep their places in the unit proper.)

Information gap The actual activities are printed with the instructions for each group or individual on different pages, so that the participants will not see each other's instructions. Don't allow students to prepare beforehand or to 'cheat' by looking at each other's instructions – the whole point of the communication activities is to *reveal* information to some students, and *withhold* it from others who must try and get it. This creates the 'information gap' or 'uncertainty' mentioned on page 2 above as one of the essential ingredients of genuine communication.

Procedure In the communication activities, you have to trust the book to control the conversation, and only step in when things are going too slowly or too fast. Try not to interrupt the flow of conversations in any way, but monitor the conversations and give help where it is needed. You may have to stop the activity at some point to make time for the very important discussion period. The students then report on what they did and you all discuss their performance – not as actors but as speakers of English. The remarks made above on the procedures for freer practice sections apply equally well to handling communication activities, particularly the remarks on monitoring the conversations, repeating activities, changing partners and recording.

Teacher's Book The complete 'route' of the communication activities for each unit is given in the Teacher's Book. There is also a brief description of the topic of each activity and a note of each student's or group's role, so that the teacher can see at a glance how the activity works. There is also a note on how to handle an extra student if you have an odd man out.

Written work

Content The written work section at the end of every unit gives more opportunities for experimenting with different ways of expressing the functions dealt with in the unit. It is intended to bring together much of what has been covered in the unit, and is a useful check on what has been mastered and where problems still lie.

Procedure It is best to discuss each piece of written work with the students before they tackle it, and to decide together on some good ways to deal with it. If you give it as homework, make sure your students all know exactly what they have to do. You may have to spend some time on mistakes when you hand the written work back – focus more on how well students have communicated their thoughts, rather than on correct grammar and spelling.

Teacher's Book The opening lines of a possible version of each written task are given in the Teacher's Book. Very often this is a good way of showing students how to start confidently – the rest is up to them. These opening lines are just suggestions – they are *not* intended to be 'models'.

Conclusion

Functions of English may be a little different from what you are used to, but since real-life communication is so often unpredictable, a course that aims to teach it must in some ways be unpredictable too. During a lesson it is important to be flexible and to allow some things to happen that you haven't planned – as long as they are within the scope of the course. In this way, the classroom communication can become even more true-to-life.

We hope that you and your students will enjoy using this book and that you will find that it helps you to stimulate each other to communicate.

1 Talking about yourself, starting a conversation, making a date

Make sure the class have read the Introduction before the first lesson – or that they read it immediately afterwards. Do they have any questions?

Functional objectives

Apart from getting to know each other better, students will improve their ability to make contact with strangers, to talk about themselves and to arrange meetings with people.

Presupposed knowledge

The necessary lexis to describe one's background, education, job and interests.
How to talk about the weather as an ice-breaking topic.

The practice activities in this unit will show the gaps in your class's knowledge. But you may like to ask around the class, making sure each student can say the name of his or her job, hobbies and educational qualifications, before you begin the unit. *Notions in English* unit 1: The weather deals with 'breaking the ice', among other things.

1.1 Conversation

Books closed. Play tape through once for 'gist'. Play again, stopping the tape after each example of the functions listed above. Ask students to tell you what the speakers said – write these examples on the board. Finally, perhaps, play the tape again and ask students to underline the examples in their books. In this transcript the examples of these functions are printed in italics. Places for you to pause are marked like this: ‖, if you want to ask the class 'What's he or she going to say next' questions.

Richard: *Excuse me, anyone sitting here?*

Jane:	Um, no, no. Oh! Er . . . I'll just move my bag.
Richard:	Right, thanks.
Jane:	There we are!
Richard:	Thank you . . . *Oh, nice day, isn't it?* ‖
Jane:	*Oh, it's lovely, yes. It does make a change, doesn't it*
Richard:	*Let's hope it'll last.*
Jane:	Mm, mm.
Richard:	What . . . *what's that book you're reading? Looks . . looks really interesting.*
Jane:	Oh, it's . . . it's called *Life on Earth*. Um, I got it because . . . er . . . because of that . . . um . . . television programme.
Richard:	Oh yeah.
Jane:	Did . . . did you see it? A few . . . a few weeks ago? ‖
Richard:	No, no, I didn't see it – I remember it, but I didn't see it, I'm afraid.
Jane:	Yes, about how life began. It's . . . it's fantastic. I'm . . . I'm reading it as well because I've got a project at school – I'm a teacher.
Richard:	I see, I see.
Jane:	And it's really useful for ‖ background research – it's lovely.
Richard:	Yes, I like . . . I like a bit of telly really. I like the old movies best of all . . .
Jane:	Oh, yes. So do I.
Richard:	The old films.
Jane:	Yes, yes. They're on very late, though. I don't see a lot of them, because . . . [*fade*]
Jane:	. . . but I don't go to the cinema a lot, there just isn't time.
Richard:	Well, I'm going tonight, in fact.
Jane:	Tonight? Oh, are you?
Richard:	Yes, most nights really.
Jane:	What are you going to see?
Richard:	The new Clint Eastwood film.
Jane:	Oh, lovely!
Richard:	*You wouldn't like to come, would you? Why don't you come as well?*
Jane:	*Oh, that would be nice, yes!* Oh, why not? . . . Oh, *oh dear, I'm busy tonight, I'm afraid. What about tomorrow night?* Is that any good to you?
Richard:	*Oh dear, no,* ‖ *I'm afraid I'm busy then myself.*
Jane:	Oh . . . well . . .

Richard: Well . . . we . . . obviously ‖ it'd be nice to meet sometime. Er . . .
Jane: Yes.
Richard: Er . . . perhaps if you gave me your phone number ‖ I could . . . we could fix something up?
Jane: Oh, yes, alright. Well, shall I write it down for you?
Richard: Sure, yes.
Jane: OK . . .
Richard: Good heavens! ‖ I should have been at the office ten minutes ago!
Jane: Oh dear.
Richard: Er, look, I'll . . . I'll . . . that's the number, is it?
Jane: Yes, here you are.
Richard: Thanks, I'll . . . I'll give you a ring then and . . . ‖ and we'll sort something out.
Jane: Alright.
Richard: Right, well, it's been very nice meeting you.
Jane: Yes!
Richard: Byebye, then!
Jane: Yes, byebye!
Richard: Byebye!

1.2 Presentation: talking about yourself

Discuss with the class the sort of questions you would ask someone you've just met to find out more about him or her. For example:

Do you live near here?
Where do you come from?
What do you do?

Point out that the pair work in the next section will enable them to relax as they speak without an audience, and to concentrate on finding things out rather than worrying about total accuracy. It also means that they are on their own to some extent – so they should call you over and ask you if they are at a loss for words or can't express themselves satisfactorily.

1.3 Practice in pairs

Sit beside a confident student and demonstrate how you want the class to continue.

Hallo. May I introduce myself – my name's Leo, what's yours? . . . Oh, I haven't heard that name before, how do you spell it? . . . Where do you come from? . . . What town do you come from? . . . Do you live in the town centre or in the suburbs? . . What sort of house do you live in? And what do you do? . . .

Be friendly and tell your partner about yourself at the same tin Before students begin working in pairs, check that they understand what they have to do. (Make one group of three if you have an odd number.)

1.4 Practice in pairs

Put students into different pairs from 1.3 (+ one group of three if necessary). As you will want to read the completed questionnaires afterwards at your leisure, it might be an idea for student to use their own paper, rather than write in their books! Go round helping each pair. Discuss the activity with the class:

Did you find it easy to fill in?
Did you and your partner fill in different things?
Was there a question you couldn't answer?
Was there any extra *information you wanted to give?*

Read (and correct) the completed questionnaires. Use the information to tailor your course to your students' needs and interests. If you plan to ignore some students' expectations, explain why you intend to do this and suggest ways in which a student with unusual needs can do extra work on his or her own profitably.

1.5 Practice as a class

Everyone stands up and circulates. If any group spends too long together, step in yourself as host or hostess and whisk guests away to another part of the party:

Now then, A, I want you to meet someone who's been dying to meet you.
Or:
A, come and meet B – I'm sure you two will have a lot in common.
Or:

A, have you met B? He comes from . . .

Afterwards, talk about the activity. If students found it difficult, find out why and offer advice.

(If there is time before the next section, ask the class to prepare it at home.)

1.6 Presentation: starting a conversation

Play the tape through once to get the general points across. Then play it again pausing for repetition and discussion of how to use each expression. Alternatively, if the class have prepared the section, ask them to give you some opening gambits. Write each one up, practise pronunciation and discuss how to use each expression. Note that all these opening gambits are really tricks, especially the last three. Ask for more ideas:

It's a beautiful day, isn't it?
Sorry to disturb you, but what's that you're drinking?
Excuse me, aren't you Mr A?
Would you like a cigarette?

To practise these opening gambits, get the class to imagine they are all sitting in a waiting room or an airport departure lounge. They should start a conversation with the 'stranger' beside them.

1.7 Communication activity in two groups

Divide the class into two groups, A and B. Make sure the students in group A all look at communication activity 151 and the students in group B look at communication activity 38. Allow time for reading and check that everyone knows what they have to do. Then tell everyone to stand up. Group A students have to start conversations with group B students. Don't let the conversations go on too long. If necessary, call out: 'Change partners!' at regular intervals. Go round the class monitoring.

When several conversations have taken place, stop this part of the activity and tell everyone in group A to look at activity 136 and everyone in group B to look at activity 16. Allow time for reading. Then group A students are approached by group B students, who will start conversations with them. Go round moni toring.

After several conversations, stop everyone and discuss the activity with the class by asking what went wrong and what wa difficult. Tell the class what you heard while you were monito ing. If necessary, 'replay' part of the activity.

In brief:
In the first part, group A look at activity 151 and group B at activity 38.
In the second part, group A look at activity 136 and group B a activity 16.
(If you have an odd number of students, so that group A is larger than group B, you may need to join in yourself as a mem ber of group B.)

1.8 Presentation: making a date

Ask for alternative ideas and write them up:

Have you got any plans for Saturday?
What are you doing at the weekend?

That sounds a very nice idea, thanks.
It's very nice of you to ask me, thanks.

I'd love to come, but the problem is . . .
I'm afraid I'm tied up tonight.
I've got to baby-sit tonight, I'm afraid.
It's really nice of you to ask, but . . .
I'd really like to, but the problem is . . .

Point out that these are *not* just pick-up techniques. They are needed for arranging to meet acquaintances and friends of eithe sex.
What you may say before: break the ice, talk about the weather introduce yourselves, discuss topics of general interest.

What you may say after: arrange time and place of meeting, or suggest another day:

Fine, let's meet outside the . . .
OK, where shall we meet?
How about tomorrow evening, then?

Could you make it next week?
Would Saturday be convenient?

1.9 Practice (pattern conversation)

This pattern conversation should begin under your close control. Check on pronunciation, tone of voice and ease of expression to begin with.
Then encourage students to:
1 Use different expressions each time.
2 Leave the pattern and improvise.
When the class seem confident, allow them to work privately in pairs. At the end, ask each pair to perform one conversation without books in front of the class. Ask for comments.

1.10 Practice as a class

An alternative to this is to give each student a slip of paper or 'role card' telling him or her what to do. The aim is to get as many acceptances as possible to your invitation. Here are some suggestions, but your own topical/local ideas are better for your class:

1 You want to have a really good meal one evening. Find a suitable evening when as many others as possible can come. Make a note of their names.
2 You want to go on a drive in the country this weekend in your car. See who else would like to come with you. Note their names.
3 You want to go to a pub for lunch tomorrow. See who else would like to come. Note their names.
4 You want to go out for a pizza for lunch tomorrow. See who else would like to come. Note their names.
5 There's a good documentary on TV tonight about your country. Find some others to watch it with you on your TV. You'll provide food and drink. Make a note of their names.
6 There's a sentimental, romantic film at the cinema. See who wants to go with you tomorrow evening. Note their names.
7 Get some people to go on a 'pub crawl' with you tomorrow evening (i.e. visiting a lot of pubs, having one drink in each). Note their names.

8 Find out who would like to go to a disco with you tonight. Note their names.
9 Find out who wants to go on a country walk with you this Sunday. Note their names.
10 There's a good orchestral concert on Thursday. Find some people to go with you (tickets are half-price for students). Note their names.
11 Get as many people as possible to go sunbathing with you on the beach at the weekend. Make a note of their names.
12 There's a James Bond film on TV this evening but you haven't got a TV set. Find out who's going to watch it and see if you can get an invitation.
13 Get some people to go to London with you at the weekend Note their names.
14 See who is interested in playing tennis this afternoon. You need three others to play doubles. Note their names.
15 There's a sexy, violent American film at the cinema. See who wants to go with you tonight. Note their names.

As this is the last oral practice section in this unit, monitor the activity carefully to assess how well the class are 'performing'. Refer back to the functional objectives – have they been achieved? Does more work need to be done on any aspect? (You may also want to discuss with the class some signals people use when they don't want to talk: turning away, giving a one-word answer, starting to read a magazine etc. How would they react to such signals?)

1.11 Written work

These suggested opening lines are *not* intended to be models. They just give an idea of one possible way of approaching each topic:

1 A: Excuse me, may I sit here?
B: Yes, of course, I'll just move my coat.
A: Thanks. Lovely day, isn't it?
B: Mm, it certainly is.
A: Would you like a cigarette?
B: Oh thanks very much.
A: These are a bit strong, I'm afraid.
B: Oh that's alright. I like strong ones . . .
etc.

2 Dear John,
As this is my first letter to you, let me begin by introducing myself and telling you something about myself. My name's A and I was born in X, though most of my childhood was spent in Y. I left school in . . . and began work for a firm of . . .

3 Dear Peter,
I expect you are a little surprised to hear from me after such a long silence. My reason for writing is to say how much I enjoyed your company and to invite you over to Z to stay with me and my family. I have told them a lot about you and they are really looking forward to meeting you . . .

2 Asking for information: question techniques, answering techniques, getting more informatio

Functional objectives

Students will extend their ability to introduce a question politely, to delay an answer or avoid reply, to press people to give more detail.

Presupposed knowledge

The form of direct and indirect questions.
Asking questions with appropriate intonation.
(Practice material in *Notions in English* unit 2: Questions; *English in Situations* B7 and C7.)

2.1 Conversation

Alternatively, if there is a student from an unusual country or with knowledge of an unusual subject, ask him or her questions about it and encourage the class to ask questions too. Point out that very direct questions may sound like a police interrogation – questions often need to be introduced politely.
In this transcript examples of the functions are printed in italics and places to pause are marked like this: ‖.

Stranger: Excuse me.
Resident: Yes?
Stranger: *I was wondering if you could help me* . . .
Resident: Well, I'll try.
Stranger: I need to find out where the . . . ‖ er . . . town centre is. Now I see there's a sign up there that points to the left.
Resident: Ah *well, let me see* . . . er . . . it all depends if you're on foot or going by car.
Stranger: Ah no, I'm walking.
Resident: Ah well, you turn to the right and then carry straight on.
Stranger: Ah, right, thanks! Er . . . *I wonder if you could tell*

	me . . . er . . . ‖ anything about the . . . er . . . castle in town . . . er . . . where . . . where it is.
Resident:	Um, well, it's actually further on . . . er . . . ‖ down the High Street and then you cross over the bridge ‖ and it's on the other side of the river.
Stranger:	I see, I see. *Could you tell me a bit more about it?* Is it interesting? Is it old?
Resident:	*I'm not really sure.* I've never actually been there myself. It . . . yes, I think it's quite old, I think it's about . . . um . . . 500 years old – something like that.
Stranger:	Worth . . . worth visiting, you think?
Resident:	Well, it's one of the ‖ tourist attractions of the town . . . um . . .
Stranger:	I see, I see.
Resident:	*I've no idea, I'm afraid.* As I say, I've never been there.
Stranger:	I see. *Do you happen to know* ‖ when it's open?
Resident:	Er . . . *I'm not really sure* . . . um . . . I think it depends on . . . er . . . ‖ what time of year you go . . . um . . . as to whether it's open.
Stranger:	Well, right, thank you, thank you.
Resident:	Er, *excuse me, I hope you don't mind my asking,* but . . . um . . . your voice interests me . . . er . . . *do you mind if I ask* . . . er . . . ‖ where you come from?
Stranger:	No, no, no. I come from Wiltshire.
Resident:	Ah!

2.2 Presentation: question techniques

The appropriateness of the listed opening expressions may depend on whether the information required is
a) Simple facts
b) Complicated, difficult to define
c) Personal, potentially embarrassing

Examples of *in*appropriate questions might be if one asked a stranger:
a) *I hope you don't mind my asking, but I'd like to know what time the London train leaves.*
b) *What's the economy of your country?*
c) *Why did you leave your wife?*

Ask for ideas on other ways to introduce a personal question:

I hope you don't think I'm being nosy, but . . .
Please don't answer this if it's too personal, but . . .

2.3 Practice as a class

Examples of factual information:
Population of Britain.
How much airline ticket to New York costs.
What's on at the cinema.

Examples of personal information:
Married?
How many children?
Where do you live?
How much do you earn?

Correct mistakes in grammar and appropriateness. Demonstrat the *delaying* techniques and *avoiding* techniques to be presente in 2.4. Make a mental note of the questions asked as ammuniti for 2.5.

2.4 Presentation: answering techniques

Ask for more ideas on how to delay your answer, such as:

Wait a minute, I'll just have a look.
I'll come back to you on that one.
Could I answer that one later, I need to look it up.

And for more ideas on what to say when you don't know the answer:

I really don't know.
I haven't a clue I'm afraid.
Do you know, I really can't remember.

or don't want to answer:

That's something I'd rather not talk about at the moment.
That'd be telling, wouldn't it?

2.5 Practice as a class

Fire embarrassing personal questions and difficult questions of fact at members of the class, for example, about their countries. Correct inappropriate replies. Suggest better ways of answering.

2.6 Communication activity in pairs

Student A: part one activity 40 part two activity 57
Student B: part one activity 109 part two activity 124
(If you have an extra student, form one group of three with two students working as A.)

In part one student B finds out from A about the Beatles' career 1956–64. A has all the facts, B has a sheet with missing information. In part two student A finds out from B about the Beatles' career 1965–70. This time B has all the facts.

Begin by reminding students that they should only look at their own page, not their partner's. Allow time for preparatory reading and questions first. Perhaps point out that although the information is in note form, the questions and answers need to be fuller sentences.
When they have finished, ask the class to report what difficulties they had in communicating and in phrasing suitable questions. Make your comments on their performance.

2.7 Presentation: getting more information

As an example, take a description of someone's job:

A: I work in an office.
B: What do you do exactly?
A: You know, I answer the phone and so on.
B: REQUEST FOR EXTRA INFORMATION

2.8 Practice as a class

Allow time for preparation. Perhaps get students to work out a few nasty questions, conspiring in pairs. Be evasive in answering. Force them to use expressions from 2.7.

2.9 Communication activity in groups of four

Student A: activity 99
Student B: activity 92
Student C: activity 44
Student D: activity 8 (can be omitted)

Each student has some information about one of the famous people on English £1, £5, £10 and £20 notes:
Student A is an expert on Sir Isaac Newton (£1).
Student B is an expert on the Duke of Wellington (£5).
Student C is an expert on Florence Nightingale (£10).
Student D is an expert on William Shakespeare (£20).

Each biography gives similar information about the person's life, what they are famous for, and some related information about the English language. The idea is for the non-experts to find out as much as possible from the expert.

Allow time for reading and questions before the activity begins. You may need to help some students. Finish by discussing what each group did.

2.10 Practice in pairs or small groups

Monitor each group carefully (perhaps record one or more groups). Report to the class afterwards and tell them how good they are at this now and what they still need to improve. Have the functional objectives been achieved?
If necessary, rearrange groups and do the activity again for improved performance.

2.11 Written work

Some possible openings:

1 Dear Sir,
I have seen your advertisement in the *Guardian* and a colleague of mine, Mr X, has recommended your hotel to me. He is a regular guest of yours. Could you please give me the following information . . .

2 Dear Michael,
It must be over three years since we last spent an evening together. I really must apologize for not having kept in touch.

Well, a lot of things have happened here in Bournemouth. For a start, I'm not only married, but I've got a little daughter. Yes, I married Mary at last and . . .

3 Getting people to do things: requesting, attracting attention, agreeing and refusing

Functional objectives

Students will extend their ability to make requests appropriately, to agree or refuse to do something, to attract someone's attention, to make an excuse or give a reason.

3.1 Conversation

Alternatively, ask members of the class to do things for you: open window, open door, fetch book, pick up pen, clean board change places etc.
In this transcript the examples of the functions are printed in italics and places to pause are marked like this: ‖.

Brenda: Ah, right, here we are!
Bob: This is the place I was telling you about.
Brenda: Yeah, *could you ask the waiter if* ‖ we can sit near the window?
Bob: Er, *yes, of course.* Er, waiter!
Waiter: Good evening, sir.
Bob: *We'd like* ‖ *to sit near the window if that's possible.*
Waiter: Er . . . Ah! . . . er . . . I'm afraid all the tables there are . . . are taken. *Would you mind sitting* near . . . nearer nearer the bar?
Bob: Oh, yes, alright. That suit you?
Brenda: Mm, fine.
Bob: Good.
Waiter: Thank you, sir.
Bob: Now let's have a . . . er . . . oh, I . . . I *don't seem to have any cigarettes on me. Have you got a cigarette, by any chance?*
Brenda: *I'm awfully sorry,* ‖ *but you see* I've given up.
Bob: Oh, you've stopped smoking at last. Well done! . . . Oh well, let's have a look at the menu, then. Um . . . oh, there isn't a menu . . . er . . . er, *do you think you could ask* the people at the next table ‖ if we could look at their menu?

Brenda: *Yes, of course. Um . . . excuse me, could you possibly* ‖ let us see your menu? Oh, they haven't got one, either.
Bob: Er. Oh, I'll . . . ‖ I'll ask these people at this table. *Um, I wonder if you could possibly* ‖ let us have a look at your menu . . . Thank you! . . . Ah, here we are, then. Now, what's on? Um . . . oh, 'Soup of the Day' – well, I wonder what that is.
Brenda: I wonder what 'Mexican Dressing' is.
Bob: Oh, sounds interesting . . . er, where's the waiter gone, we'll order . . . er . . . I can't see . . . ‖
Brenda: He's over there.
Bob: Oh, *could you possibly* ‖ *catch his eye?*
Brenda: Yeah. Um, waiter!
Waiter: Yes, madam.
Bob: Ah, waiter . . . um, *I wonder if you could tell me* ‖ what 'Soup of the Day' is, please.
Waiter: Certainly, yes. 'Soup of the Day' is Cream of Asparagus.
Bob: Ah, that sounds nice!
Brenda: Mm, *could you tell me* ‖ what 'Mexican Dressing' is?
Waiter: Ah, 'Mexican Dressing', yes. That's one of our specialities. That's hot, spicy and sweet. It's very nice, I recommend it.
Brenda: Oh!
Waiter: Er . . . now . . . *could I . . . I wonder if I could possibly ask you to* ‖ move to a table near the window after all? It's . . . er . . . it turns out the manager tells me ‖ this table's reserved.
Brenda: *Oh, yes, sure.*
Bob: *Of course, by all means.*

3.2 Presentation: requesting

Perhaps begin by asking the students what's wrong with the words used by the people in the cartoons.
Examples of different types of tasks:
Open window
Go down to town to buy something
Telephone somebody for you

Examples of different roles and relationships:
strangers
good friends
colleagues

headmaster
child
boss

Good friends can use the least polite forms, even when the request may be difficult to fulfil:

You haven't got 5 quid, have you?
Hey, I need some money.

Ask for other ways to make requests:

* *Can you . . .*
* *I want you to . . .*
** *Would you please . . .*
***** *I'm sorry to trouble you, but is there any chance of your . . .-ing for me please?*

Note that adding a *'please'* has the effect of adding a 'politeness star'. Note also that an inappropriate tone of voice can remove several stars. Too polite an expression can sound sarcastic (very rude):

I wonder if you could possibly manage to arrive earlier next time?

3.3 Practice as a class

A bag or box of props is helpful here. Students can then actually ask you to really give them things. The props may include:
pens, paper, rubber, scissors etc.
coins and real or play money
books, newspapers, magazines
mirror, comb, nailfile etc.

Correct inappropriate requests (or pretend to be offended by rudeness). Agree appropriately to do the things you are requested to do.

3.4 Communication activity in pairs around the class

Student A: part one activity 80 part two activity 110
Student B: part one activity 47 part two activity 25
(An extra student can be A or B.)

Allow time for thinking, then in part one all student As stand up and go round the classroom asking each student B to do something different for them. In part two, the student Bs do the asking.

Monitor what goes on, paying particular attention to appropriateness. Afterwards report to the class how well or badly they performed. Do the activity again if necessary.

3.5 Practice as a class

Play each of the different roles – each for a few minutes. Make it crystal clear which role you're playing – react to requests in character with the role you're playing. Step out of role to correct inappropriate requests.

3.6 Communication activity in pairs around the class

Student A: part one activity 41 part two activity 123
Student B: part one activity 61 part two activity 85
(An extra student can be A or B.)

In part one, all student As have a list of requests, all student Bs have to select a role and make a badge or label to identify themselves to others. Make sure there are several different roles amongst the student Bs. In part two the situations are reversed. All students should stand up during this activity.

Monitor appropriateness. If necessary, stop everyone and make them start again. Discuss their success at the end.

3.7 Presentation: attracting attention, agreeing and refusing

Ask for other ideas:

To attract someone's attention:

Um . . .
(Cough)
Oh, John, . . .

To agree:

Yes, alright.
Well, alright, I suppose so.
Certainly, yes.

To refuse:

Certainly not! (Rude)
I'd rather not if you don't mind.
I certainly will not!! (Rude)

Discuss possible excuses for not wanting to lend money:

Sorry, I'm a bit short, myself.
I haven't got any change on me.

3.8 Practice (pattern conversation)

Check tone of voice first as students perform in front of the class. When ready, encourage them to work privately in pairs using a variety of expressions and excuses, and then to leave the pattern and improvise. After that, ask for a public performance of one conversation from each pair.

3.9 Communication activity in pairs around the class

Student A: part one activity 53 part two activity 150
Student B: part one activity 1 part two activity 108
(An extra student can be A or B.)

In part one all student As have a list of requests which they must get a student B (a 'stranger') to agree to before they can move on. The student Bs (who remain seated) have a list of possible excuses, though they must decide whether to agree to or refuse each request. Part two reverses the situation.

Monitor and comment on their performance.

3.10 Communication activity in pairs around the class

There are three separate situations, each of which requires one student to ask for help while the other two are in a position to agree (or refuse) to help.

Part one: Hotel robbery at 6 a.m.
Student A: activity 93
Students B and C: activity 17

Part two: Assigning the day's work in an office
Student B: activity 69
Students A and C: activity 100

Part three: Organizing a big picnic
Student C (or A in group of two): activity 132
Students B and A: activity 2

After finishing each part discuss the situation as a class before moving on to the next part.

Monitor (and perhaps record one or two groups) and report to the class on the quality of their English performance. Have the functional objectives been achieved?

3.11 Written work

Some possible beginnings:

1 Dear Uncle Alan,
I am writing to you to say how much I enjoyed the week I spent last summer at your villa in Cannes. I really had a very enjoyable time. Since then my luck has changed and the worst thing is the accident I had in my car. I believe my father told you about it . . .

2 Dear Johnny,
I am very sorry to have to tell you that I am unable to lend you the £5000 you asked for. I can see, of course, that the accident was only partly your fault but there is no excuse for not having insured the car. It is time you found out that . . .

3 A: Excuse me!
B: Yes, what's the matter? Why are you knocking at this time in the morning?
A: Well, I'm very sorry, but you see I've just been robbed.
B: Robbed! How did it happen?
A: I was just having a bath and . . .

4 Talking about past events: remembering, describing experiences, imagining 'What if . . .'

Functional objectives

Students will extend their ability to help other people to remember their past activities and talk about them, to talk about their own experiences, to speculate what might have happened otherwise.

Presupposed knowledge

Common irregular verb forms.
The use and form of simple past, past continuous, present perfect and past perfect interrogatives and statements.
Using the past conditional to make hypothetical statements about the past.
(*Notions in English* unit 6: The past, unit 11: If and unit 33: Sequence of events; *English in Situations* B4, C4 and C10.)
(Note that unit 14: Telling a story continues the theme of this unit.)

4.1 Conversation

Alternatively, tell the class about one of your own experiences, encouraging them to ask you questions. You could record this as it happens or get someone to interview you on tape before the lesson.

4.2 Presentation: remembering

These question forms can be practised by getting the class to imagine what they would ask Jane in 4.1 or you if you told them about one of your experiences. Demonstrate the use of the '*As far as I remember . . .* ' remarks as you answer.

4.3 Practice as a class

Correct and encourage a variety of expressions.

4.4 Communication activity in pairs

Student A: activity 23
Student B: activity 79
(An extra student can work as a team with A.)

Each student has a diary page which outlines what happened to him or her on Friday 13 March. First A has to find out what B did that day, then B has to find out what A did. There may be some argument towards the end! Point out that A and B are 'acquaintances', not friends.

Discuss the activity afterwards.

4.5 Practice in small groups

Perhaps demonstrate by getting one group to find out about *your* last holiday, while the others listen in.

4.6 Presentation: describing experiences

Demonstrate the use of the questions by asking the class about:
exams they have taken
countries they have visited
competitions they have entered
crimes or accidents or disasters

Note that *'Have you ever . . . ?'* is often answered with *past* forms:

Yes I have. I went *there in 1974 and I . . .*

Ask for other ideas for beginning an account of an experience:

It seems like only yesterday . . .
It's so long ago I can hardly remember . . .

4.7 Practice in groups of three or four

Monitor and report to the class what went right and wrong. Ask each group to report back what they found out.

4.8 Presentation: imagining 'What if . . .'

Practise by asking the class what they would have done if they:
hadn't come to the English lesson
had had an accident on the way here
had found some money in the street
had found the building locked today

And perhaps ask them to imagine *you* are the girl in the picture in their book. Use the prompts below in this drill:

Teacher: I saw a lovely flower.
Student: What might have happened if you hadn't seen the flower?
Teacher: I wouldn't have fallen off the cliff.

I climbed the cliff.
I wore the wrong shoes.
I lost my balance.
I slipped.
I fell 10 metres.
I broke my leg.
I was taken to hospital.
I felt better later.
I couldn't go on holiday.

It might be worth pointing out that many British people nowadays say: *'If I'd've known . . . '* and *'If he'd've told me . . . '*, but this is not acceptable in writing (or exams).

4.9 Practice as a class

Ask the class to suggest several different places in the world with different cultures, standards of living, climates etc. Correct errors and encourage the class to use their imagination. Perhaps get them to prepare in small groups first, each group concentrating on a different country.

4.10 Practice in groups of three or four

Encourage them to imagine the chain of events that might or might not have occurred, rather than simply how life would be different today. Perhaps ask the class to suggest some more events or discoveries which have changed the course of history or the way we live. Ask each group to report back.

4.11 Practice in small groups

Monitor and report back to the class how well they have mastered the expressions introduced in this unit. Have the functional objectives been achieved?

4.12 Written work

Some suggested first lines:

1 Dear John,
I simply must tell you about a fantastic trip I went on last Saturday. I met Alan and Nora at the bus station and we caught the 10 o'clock bus to Salisbury. The journey was really nice – we had a great view from the top deck and . . .

2 (The photos show: Paul Newman, Margaret Thatcher, Raquel Welch and Prince Charles.)
If I'd met Paul Newman, I would have asked him a lot of questions. First of all, I'd have asked him what it was like to be really famous – so everyone recognized you in the street. I'd have invited him to . . .

3 I'll never forget the day I took my driving test for the first time. I must say I was really nervous about it – my hands were shaking. The first thing the examiner asked was about the Highway Code; it was an easy question but my mind went blank . . .

5 Conversation techniques: hesitating, preventing interruptions and interrupting politely, bringing in other people

Functional objectives

Students will extend their ability to use a variety of hesitation devices, to make sure they are allowed to continue speaking, to interrupt politely and to encourage other speakers to take part in a discussion. (These techniques lead on to unit 8: Giving opinions, agreeing and disagreeing, discussing.)

5.1 Conversation

Alternatively, start speaking on a topical subject yourself and hesitate excessively. Perhaps record your speech and play it back for analysis. Or record any discussion between native speakers. Note that an impromptu informal conversation is likely to be more hesitant than a prepared formal discussion, where the speakers have rehearsed their points in previous discussions.

5.2 Presentation: hesitating

Note that some of these hesitation devices have 'real' meanings as well:

He's not Scottish, actually, he's Welsh.
It's over there, you see?

Ask for other hesitation devices:

as a matter of fact
kind of
the-the-the (repetition)
in-in-in (repetition)

Point out that hesitating is a necessary part of taking part in conversations, which are normally unrehearsed and unpredictable; hesitation gives you time to arrange your thoughts and to choose your words.

5.3 Practice as a class

Alternatively, put these subjects and others onto cards and get each student to pick a card at random and then immediately start speaking. The game 'Just a Minute' requires speakers to talk for one minute without 1 stopping, 2 repeating, 3 deviating from the subject, 4 hesitating – but ignore this rule here!

Further subjects for the cards might be:

The police	Motorways	Tea
Dinner	Why I like Britain	Coffee
Soup	Why I hate Britain	Hair
Soap	Language laboratories	Windows
Gas	Cats	Pop music

Correct errors and encourage students to use a variety of hesitation devices.

5.4 Presentation: preventing interruptions and interrupting politely

Demonstrate yourself, first by using the 'you can't interrupt' techniques and challenging the class to interrupt. Then by getting a group of students to start talking and trying to interrupt them yourself.

Ask for other ideas on interrupting:

If I could just butt in . . .
There's just one more point I'd like to make . . .

5.5 Communication activity in groups of three or four

Student A:	part one activity 50	part two activity 98
Student B:	part one activity 20	part two activity 133
Student C:	part one activity 74	part two activity 10
Student D:	part one activity 107	part two activity 39

(Student D can be omitted)

In each part, each student is looking at a different aspect of the same general area. They are given a point of view which they have to justify to the others and make them listen to:

Part one: Smokers' rights
A: No smoking in public places.
B: No interference in personal liberty.
C: Smoking should be illegal.
D: Cigarettes should be taxed higher.

Discuss their performance in part one before going on.

Part two: Work
A: Workers need longer holidays.
B: Workers don't work hard enough.
C: Machines should do routine jobs.
D: Automation means unemployment.

Discuss the activity afterwards and report on your monitoring.

5.6 Presentation: bringing in other people

Demonstrate by starting a conversation with one student, then bring in another student, then another until the conversation snowballs to include everyone.

5.7 Practice in groups of four or five

Monitor and check that the reticent students are brought into the first discussion. Report to the class and offer advice before they start the second discussion.

5.8 Communication activity in three groups

Group A: activity 35
Group B: activity 75
Group C: activity 101

Each group or 'committee' has to prepare a report to the rest of the class on:

A: Their main difficulties with English vocabulary
B: Their main difficulties with English grammar
C: Their main difficulties with English pronunciation

Listen carefully to each report – it may be enlightening. Ask the groups to comment on each other's reports.
Have the functional objectives been achieved?

5.9 Written work

Some possible openings:

1 A: Hallo, John.
B:
A: Very well thank you. What sort of day did you have yesterday?
B:
A: Really? I don't believe it.
B:
A: Alright. I'll take your word for it. What happened exactly?
B:

2 A:
B: Hallo Alan, how are you?
A:
B: Great! You know that car I was thinking of buying – well, – I bought it!
A:
B: It's true, it's true. And, you know, it was a real bargain.
A:
B: Well, actually . . .

3 Dear John,

Look, I'm ever so sorry I couldn't make our date yesterday. You see, the thing is that I met my old teacher. You know, Mr Jones. And we sort of began talking and before I realized it, I'd actually missed my bus . . .

6 Talking about the future: stating intentions, discussing probability, considering 'What if . . .'

Functional objectives

Students will extend their ability to say how firmly they intend to do something, to say how likely events are to happen, to consider what might happen if the future were different from what is expected.

Presupposed knowledge

The use of *will*, *shall*, *going to*, *may*, *might* and *could* to refer to future.
The use of simple present in time clauses referring to the future.
How to make hypothetical statements using the conditional.
(*Notions in English* unit 10: The future, unit 11: If and unit 19: Possibility; *English in Situations* B3 and C3.)

6.1 Conversation

Alternatively, tell the class about your own holiday plans and ask them about theirs. Emphasize the degree of confidence you have in various plans (see 6.2 and 6.7).

6.2 Presentation: stating intentions

Demonstrate the use of the expressions by talking about your own plans for the evening – both what you intend to do and what you don't intend to do. Then ask the class to talk about their plans.

6.3 Practice as a class

Give the class time to check the lists and mark them. Then ask each student to speak about his or her intentions. For variety, it might be nice to ask them *'Why?'* sometimes.

6.4 Practice in small groups

Perhaps first ask each student to draw a sketch map of his country and put in the names of the neighbouring countries. This will help them to concentrate. (If most of your students never travel abroad, ask them to talk about different parts of their own country.)

6.5 Communication activity in three groups

Group A: activity 31
Group B: activity 3
Group C: activity 143

Each group is asked to plan a journey and decide what they are going to take. If a group disagrees about the necessity of an item, then it's something they will *perhaps* or *probably* take or not take. If they all agree, then they'll *definitely* take it or not take it. Each group reports to the whole class at the end.

Group A are going by car from Algiers to Cape Town.
Group B are going to sail round the world by yacht.
Group C are going on a bicycle tour of Europe.

Monitor each group and offer advice on needed vocabulary.

6.6 Practice in small groups

Monitor and throw in ideas to keep the conversation going. Encourage students to use a variety of recommended expressions – interrupt and ask them to start again if necessary.

6.7 Presentation: discussing probability

Demonstrate each expression by talking about tomorrow's weather or next month's weather.
Note that a 'tentative' tone of voice (as opposed to a 'confident' tone of voice) shows a lack of certainty when we talk about events that will perhaps happen. Note also that over-confidence is often seen as pomposity or even bluff!
It's also important to make sure that the students can use the correct *short* answers to the question: *'Do you think it'll . . . ?'*

✓ *Of course it will.*
It's sure to.
It's bound to.

✓? *I expect so.*
I wouldn't be surprised if it did.
I bet it will.

?? *There's a chance it will.*
It might possibly.
I suppose it might.

✗? *I doubt if it will.*
I don't think so.
There's not much chance.

✗ *Of course not.*
There's no chance.
I'm absolutely sure it won't.

6.8 Practice in small groups

Madame Zoë knows what will happen in the future. Demonstr how each group should deal with her predictions:

She says that . . . but I'd say there's not much chance of it happening then. Of course there's a chance it'll happen sometime this century – in fact I wouldn't be surprised if it happened . . years from now . . .

Ask for a report from each group.

6.9 Practice in three groups

Perhaps look at the items together as a class and agree on the average price of each one today. Add some other items of gene interest to the list. Then ask each group to look into their economic inflationary crystal balls and predict the prices in five years' time. Then the groups are shuffled so that each new grou has former members of each of the first groups – they argue about or discuss their original estimates.

6.10 Practice in groups

Perhaps start the ball rolling by talking as a class about changes that have taken place in the past fifteen years. Talk briefly about politics, science and technology, economic affairs and everyday life. Ask each group to decide on their predictions before they report back to the whole class.

6.11 Presentation: considering 'What if . . .'

Demonstrate by saying what you would do/how you would feel/what it would be like if *you* became a millionaire. Ask the class to make their own suggestions.
Point out the essential difference between *extremely unlikely* and *possible* future events (as expressed by 'conditional II' and 'conditional I' respectively).
If necessary, practise speculating about *possible* future events and their consequences by asking the class to invent sentences from these prompts:
nice summer
bad winter
further inflation
election results
TV programme
enough time
enough money

For example:

A: If we have a nice summer this year, how will you feel?
B: Oh, I'll be really pleased.

Note that a useful 'rule of thumb' to spot a *possible* future event is the use of: *'It all depends on . . . '* as in:
It all depends on the weather. If it's fine, we'll go out. If it rains we'll stay in.

6.12 Practice (pattern conversation)

Perhaps remind the class that all the events in the prompts are either impossible or extremely unlikely.
Correct errors of pronunciation and grammar. Encourage students to use a variety of expressions and to leave the pattern and improvise later.

6.13 Practice in small groups

Monitor and encourage each group. Ask them what they would *miss* most.

At the report stage, perhaps use the 'Desert Island Discs' idea (the radio programme which each week asks a celebrity which eight records he would take if he were cast away on a desert island). But instead of just records, ask the class what books, food, clothes, luxuries, other person they would want to have with them – and why. And would they try to escape – if so, how?

6.14 Communication activity in small groups

1 First each group has to decide on their plans for the next few days and their ambitions for the future.
2 Then, and not until then, allow them to look at activity 9. (This tells them to speculate how their short-term plans would change if they were cut off by snow-drifts.)
3 Then allow them to look at activity 58 (which introduces the unlikely possibility that they never need to work again).
4 Discuss the whole practice with the class.

6.15 Written work

Some possible openings:

1 Dear Mary,
You told me about your own holiday plans over the phone the other day. Now I've been thinking and trying to decide what to do myself. I haven't made up my mind whether to go abroad yet. If I do go abroad, I may well go on a package holiday to Spain again . . .

2 *The world in 2100*
I'll try to make this prediction seem as realistic as possible – but looking this far ahead is really just like science fiction. To begin with there is likely to be some sort of world government by then, probably not a democracy but a military dictatorship. Life is sure to be much less free than it is now, for example . . .

3 If I became President, the first thing I'd do would be to abolish the armed forces. I'd keep a strong police force to

maintain internal security and prevent the Opposition from taking over. In fact I'd probably deport all the Opposition to another country, so that all the people in my country supported me. The next thing I'd do would be to . . .

7 Offering to do something, asking permission, giving reasons

Functional objectives

Students will extend their ability to offer to do things themselves for other people, to get others to allow them to do something, to give or refuse permission, to explain why they want to do something.

Presupposed knowledge

How to make requests appropriately (as practised in *Functions of English* unit 3: Getting people to do things).
How to explain causes and consequences.
How to make excuses.
(*Notions in English* unit 36: Reasons.)

7.1 Conversation

Alternatively, go round the class helpfully offering to do things for individual students, like opening windows, lending pens, books etc., looking at written work. And ask their permission to do various things, like leaving the room, sitting down, missing the next lesson. Give your reasons for each.

7.2 Presentation: offering to do something

Ask for other ways of offering:

I'll get it for you.
Here, let me help you.

and accepting:

Yes, please.
Thanks very much indeed.

and refusing:

No, it's fine, don't worry.
Thanks a lot, but I'm OK.

Practise by telling the class you need various things: pen, paper, book, cassette recorder, paper clip, dictionary, board pen or chalk, drink etc.
Get them to offer to lend, fetch or give you what you need. Refuse or accept each offer.

7.3 Practice as a class

Tell the class your problems – the practice is more productive if you really act the part! Get them to make offers of help – not suggestions of what you should do but ways they can help. Correct errors.
Continue in pairs if more practice is needed and perhaps ask each pair to perform with the rest of the class listening. Ask for comments.

7.4 Communication activity in pairs

Student A: activity 91
Student B: activity 63
(An extra student can share A's problems.)

Student A begins by telling B each of the problems in his or her list and waiting for an offer of help. Then A hears about B's problems.

7.5 Presentation: asking permission

Examples of (a): opening window if the room is cold *or* stuffy, borrowing a pen *or* a car, leaving five minutes early *or* thirty minutes early.
Examples of (b): boss, teacher, colleague, best friend.

Decide with the class which expression would be appropriate for each combination of the examples.

Ask for other ideas for giving permission:

Yes, of course you can, go ahead!
By all means.

and refusing permission:

No you can't do that! (very rude)
I'm afraid that's not really possible.
I'm sorry, but that's quite out of the question.
Well, if you did that . . . (+ unpleasant consequences)

7.6 Practice as a class

Allow each student time to make a list of five things.
The class then ask you for permission and, if relevant, you ask them why they want to do these things.
Then leave the room and come back in the role of principal (or director of studies or headmaster or headmistress). Perhaps wear a different coat.
Correct errors by stepping out of the role.

7.7 Presentation: giving reasons

Decide with the class how they might explain their reasons for wanting to borrow your: pen, watch, shoes, book, jacket, comb keys etc.

7.8 Practice (pattern conversation)

Correct errors and offer advice.

7.9 Communication activity in pairs

Student A: part one activity 11 part two activity 84
Student B: part one activity 56 part two activity 114
(An extra student can share B's part.)

In part one, student B plays in quick succession the roles of friend, teacher and boss while student A has to ask each 'character' for permission to do various things. Both A and B must do the conversations in the order given in the instructions. In part two, the roles are reversed. Again the sequence must be followed.

Monitor for appropriate language and report to the class afterwards.

7.10 Communication activity in groups of three

Student A: activity 105
Student B: activity 73
Student C: activity 19
(An extra student can be a B or C.)

Each 'friend' wants to do so certain things to help A, who also wants to do certain things. Make sure each student makes a private list *before* the groups meet. Perhaps circulate making suggestions.

Monitor and report to the class afterwards.

7.11 Written work

Some possible openings:

1 Dear Michael,
Congratulations on your new job in Uganda! I know you haven't got much time before you have to leave so perhaps I could help. You'll be leaving your flat, so would you like me to help you pack up your books? If you like I could store them in my attic. Oh, and let me help you with . . .

2 Dear Sir,
I am writing to you on behalf of my class A79 at the English Language Study College. We should like to hold a barbecue in Queen's Park and I have been told that we need to be given permission by the Park Superintendant. The date we have in mind is . . .

3 Dear Rob,
You may remember that when we last met I asked you about your cottage in Sturminster Marshall and you very kindly offered to let me use it for a weekend. I must say I've been really looking forward to having an opportunity to take you up on your offer. I wonder if it would be possible to borrow the keys on . . .

8 Giving opinions, agreeing and disagreeing, discussing

Functional objectives

Students will extend their ability to introduce their opinions, t agree or disagree with other people's opinions, to express opinions tentatively, to ask other people to explain their point of view.

Presupposed knowledge

Conversation techniques practised in *Functions of English* unit 5.

8.1 Conversation

Alternatively, begin discussing a topic in today's news (perhaps after playing a recording of today's radio news). Introduce you own opinions and ask the class to say what they think.

8.2 Presentation: giving opinions

Ask for other ideas:

As far as I'm concerned . . .
It seems quite clear to me that . . .
Well, obviously . . .
I can't help thinking that . . .

Note that the more informal expressions are appropriate for friendly relationships, and the more formal ones for talking to strangers and people older than or senior to yourself.

8.3 Practice (pattern conversation)

Perhaps run through the conversations twice – once with A and B as friends, then again with A and B pretending to be strangers.

8.4 Practice in groups of three

Monitor and offer advice. Get each group to join up with another group at the end and exchange opinions.

8.5 Presentation: agreeing and disagreeing

Ask for more ideas on how to agree, such as:

Quite right!
That's absolutely true!
I couldn't have put it better myself!

and on how to disagree, such as:

I suppose that's true in a way, but . . .
Yes, but isn't it also true to say that . . .
I suppose you could say that, but . . .

Note the danger of disagreeing directly except with close friends. Strangers and acquaintances are likely to be quite upset if you say:

No, you're wrong!
I entirely disagree!
That's just nonsense!
I don't agree at all!

8.6 Practice (pattern conversation)

Perhaps run through the conversations, twice – once with A and B pretending to be strangers, then again as friends. Or change the relationship half-way through the conversations.

8.7 Communication activity in groups of three

Student A: activity 70
Student B: activity 30
Student C: activity 7
(An extra student can share A, B or C's part.)

Each student is given two strongly held opinions while the others listen and react appropriately. Each group must follow the sequence of instructions in the activities.

8.8 Presentation: discussing

To practise these language items, take a topic from today's ne (perhaps record the radio news and listen to it first).
Point out also that we sometimes present both sides of an argu ment using expressions like:

On the one hand . . . on the other hand . . .
Although it's true to say that . . . it's also true to say that . . .

8.9 Communication activity in pairs

Student A: activity 142
Student B: activity 102
(An extra student can team up with A or B – in fact A could b a team of two and B a team of two, thus making groups of fou

Each student needs time to prepare his or her case, before the discussion begins. Then A introduces the topic of 'Exams' and puts the case for and against while B listens and reacts. Then B introduces the topic of 'Marriage'. Point out that students should give their *own* views on the topics.

Monitor and report on the class's performance.

8.10 Practice in large groups

A large class can be divided into several groups, a small class could work as one group. Each group can select a different top. The notes required are in preparation for 8.12 written work (2). These notes might take the form of:

1 Points which everyone agreed with
2 Points there was disagreement about (listing both sides' opinions)
3 Examples given
4 Conclusions of the discussion

8.11 Practice: debate as a class

Decide on a mutually interesting motion with the class. It may be best for speakers to prepare their speeches in advance at home; or small groups can prepare speeches in class before the debate begins. Select a chairman (ideally a reliable student rather than you: you will need to monitor). Appoint opening speakers for each side.

I hope you can find a topical motion, but here is a suggestion: 'This house believes that the punishment should fit the crime.' (Perhaps outline the implications of such a viewpoint on crimes like murder, terrorism and mugging. And describe the traditional notion of 'an eye for an eye, a tooth for a tooth'.)

8.12 Written work

Some possible openings:

1 *To whom it may concern*
Hans Dupont has been a student of mine since 1977. Throughout the time I have known him I have been constantly impressed by his hard work and intelligence. He has been a valuable member of his class, unselfishly helping his classmates and participating actively in lessons. His written work has improved greatly and is now . . .

2 The discussion began with general agreement that governments need to co-operate on the pollution problem. It was noted that many countries pollute international waters, the air and rivers which are shared with other countries. The Mediterranean was taken as an example. A stated that it was already a dead sea, but B disagreed and said that if action were taken quickly, the sea could be saved . . .

3 We have spent a lot of time discussing the subject of . . . I would like to put my thoughts about it on paper. First of all, I believe that . . . if only because . . . Secondly, it must be emphasized that . . . and that . . .

9 Describing things, instructing people how to do things, checking understanding

Functional objectives

Students will extend their ability to describe objects, to give people step-by-step instructions, to check that they have been clearly understood, to encourage someone following their instructions, and also to interrupt and ask for more explanatio if instructions are not understood.

9.1 Conversation

Alternatively, describe your own cassette recorder to the class (leave it outside *or* put it behind you so the class can see it but you can't). Then explain how it works, without touching or pointing at the controls.

(Note that in fact we often do point and touch things. We also say as we *show* someone how to do something: *'You do this. Then this. Then this. And this happens . . .* ' This unit, however practises the language needed for giving instructions more fully

9.2 Presentation: describing things

Ask for suggestions from the class on how to describe different objects. A box of props is essential here. It could contain all sorts of objects such as: rubber stamp, alarm clock, gloves, tickets, bottles, pencil sharpener, rubber etc.

Size – general impression: *tiny, enormous, miniscule . . .* and height, width, depth, length etc.: *5 cm high* × *(by) 10 cm wide* × *15 cm deep*
Shape: *square, circular, rectangular, oval . . .*
Colour: *greenish, bluish, sort of browny-red, sort of reddish-brown . . . crimson, navy blue, royal blue . . .*
What's it made of?: *plastic, aluminium, stainless steel, leather . .*
What does it look like?: *it looks a bit like a tube, like a box, like a transparent envelope . . .*

What's it used for?: *for attaching papers together, for telling the time, to keep sunlight out of a room . . .*
How does it work?: *you turn the knob on the back to set it and press the button on the top to turn it off . . .*

With the class look at each of the objects in your box and around you in the classroom. Write on the board the useful new words they need to describe each one. Allow the class time to make notes.
A game to practise this: Fill a bag with some mystery objects. Each student is asked to *feel* inside the bag and describe what he or she is touching. The others have to listen and guess what each object is.

9.3 Practice as a class

Alternatively, try this *game*: Write the names of many different objects on cards (or slips of paper) and ask each student to select a card at random. He or she then has to describe the object without revealing either its name or its use. The idea of the game is to describe the object perfectly truthfully but to withhold any information which will 'give the game away'. The others have to listen and guess afterwards.
Here are some objects which could go onto the cards (add more ideas of your own):

coat hanger	staple
screw	rubber band
record	bath
sunglasses	alarm clock
scissors	light bulb
armchair	frying pan
paper clip	pencil sharpener

Correct and offer suitable vocabulary to help.

9.4 Practice as a class

Allow some time for silent thinking first. Each student should be encouraged to ask about objects they really do want to know the English word for *and* objects they know the word for, but think others in the class may not know.
Go round the class getting each student to ask questions.

9.5 Practice in pairs

Perhaps suggest an example of each to start them off:
a toaster
a comb
a sock
a pen
chewing gum

Alternatively, this *game* needs a certain amount of preparation but is very useful and quite challenging:
Divide the class into pairs. Student A has a set of twelve cards and student B has a 'plan' showing how the cards must be arranged which student A must not be able to see. The cards must be arranged in exactly the same order and the same way up as shown on the plan. Each card must be accurately described by the plan-holder. The plan-holder is not allowed to point and the card-holder is not allowed to ask simply 'Where do I put this one?'
After the cards have been correctly laid out, A and B reverse roles: A gets the plan and turns it sideways, being careful not to let B see it. B shuffles the cards and they play the game again. After that, each pair swaps cards and plan with the next pair and they continue the game.
The 'cards' are easily prepared using two sheets of plain paper with carbon paper between. Divide the sheets into twelve equal squares using a ruler.
Draw *similar but subtly different* abstract designs on each square:

squiggles stripes dots

zigzags diagonal lines

and other shapes!

Cut up *one* of the finished sheets and number each card to identify it as part of set 1. Do the same with different designs to complete more sets.

Monitor and answer questions. Note that ways of expressing position may need to be revised first:

Plan

Set of cards

upside down
the other way up
in the top left-hand corner
at the bottom of the second column
on the right of the middle row

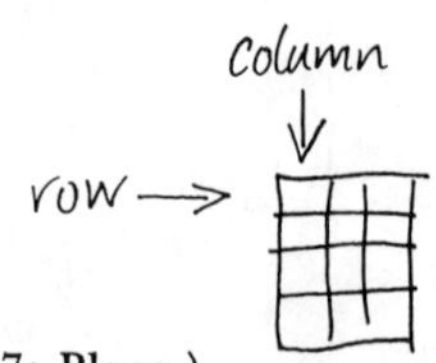

(More games in *Notions in English* unit 17: Place.)

9.6 Presentation: instructing people how to do things

Point out that written instructions can be much briefer than spoken instructions (because we can re-read sentences several times if we don't understand the first time). Written instruction are often in the form of simple lists, e.g.:

1 Plug into socket.
2 Switch on mains and on/off switch.
3 Place cassette inside flap.
  N.B. Make sure that it's the right way up!
4 Check that it's working by doing a test run.

Demonstrate by devising a list of instructions for using your classroom tape recorder and then transform them into spoken instructions.

9.7 Practice as a class

Perhaps get the class to begin as pairs to decide together what gadget they are going to explain. They could make brief notes to start with. When they are ready, ask each student to explain how his or her gadget works. Before each one starts, identify the role you will be playing:
a less mechanically-minded person than you really are
an old lady
a child
a know-all
their boss

Ask the class to comment on how the instructions *differ* when one is talking to different sorts of people.
Correct them on *inappropriate* language.

9.8 Communication activity in pairs

Student A: activity 52 (making tea)
Student B: activity 104 (making your own yogurt)
(An extra student can share A or B's part.)

First of all, A is an expert on making tea and has to tell B (who 'knows nothing about the subject') the best method. Then B tells A how to make yogurt.

Monitor and report afterwards. If necessary ask them to do it again.

9.9 Presentation: checking understanding

Ask for other ways to check understanding, such as:

Have you got all that?
Are you following me?

Perhaps get some more examples of ways for the listener to interrupt when he or she doesn't fully understand:

I didn't catch that last part.
Hold on a minute.
I don't quite follow.

Demonstrate various ways of checking understanding by telling the class how to treat flu. Include some unusual remedies to provoke interruptions for clarification. You might begin like this:

'If you think you've got flu coming on, the first thing you ought to do is go home and rest – alright so far? Fine, then you should go into the kitchen and boil a kettle . . . '

(interruption) *'Sorry, but I don't quite see why you have to boil a kettle.'*

'Ah well that's because you need a hot drink – it helps you to relax, you see. Is that clear? Right, now the best way to prepare a relaxing drink is to mix a quarter of a cup of brandy with the juice of a lemon, and then add sugar to taste and fill the cup up with boiling water . . . '

Ask the class to explain how to lay out a personal letter and a business letter. Follow their instructions and draw their suggested layout on the board:

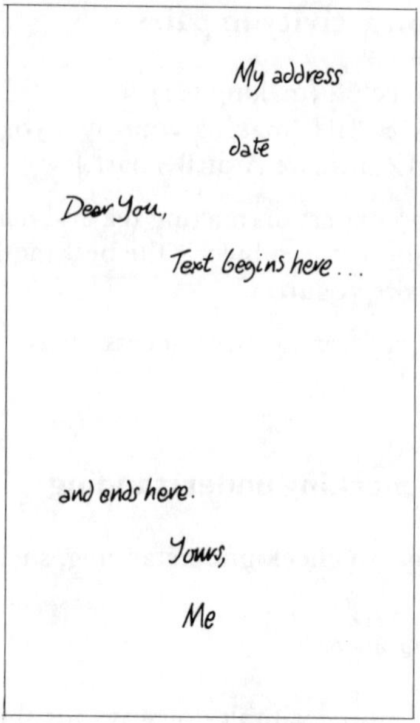

My address date Dear You, Text begins here . . . and ends here. Yours, Me	our address your name your title your address — date Dear Mr ..., Text begins here ... and ends here. Yours sincerely, Me

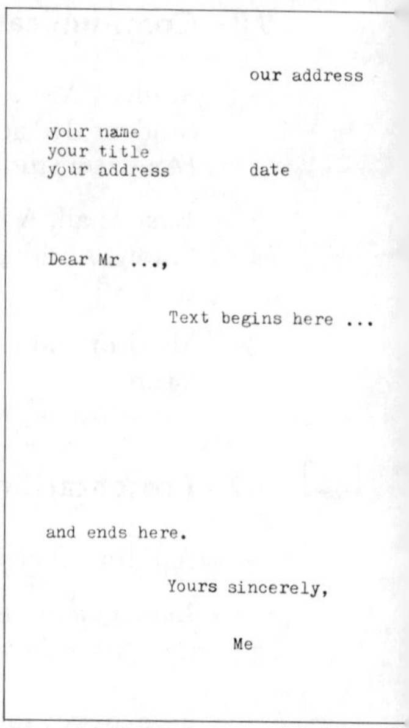

You could also ask for suggestions for the text of a 'keeping in touch' letter and an acknowledgement of receipt of goods letter

Further ideas for controlled practice:

How to use an electric typewriter or mixer or drill
How to treat a broken arm or leg
How to treat a sprained ankle or a cut finger
How to look after someone who has fainted or feels dizzy

9.10 Communication activity: in pairs first and later in groups of four

Group A: activity 51
Group B: activity 82
(With an odd number of students, the extra one can become a third member of any pair. An extra pair has to be split between two other pairs.)

Students begin working in pairs. They need enough time to write out their instructions for each of the two activities. Later each pair from group A joins up with a pair from group B, forming a group of four.

Group A are asked to work out instructions on:
1 How to play your favourite indoor game
and 2 How to make a good cup of coffee
Group B are asked to work out instructions on:
1 How to cook a favourite dish
and 2 How to play your favourite outdoor sport.

Monitor and offer advice and needed vocabulary.

9.11 Practice as a class or in large groups

Perhaps ask the class to prepare at home their explanation of 2 'An activity . . . ' Demonstrate 1 by telling them how to get to your home.
Monitor and report on the class's performance. Ask them to make their *own* comments on their performance.

9.12 Written work

Some possible opening lines:

1 It's made of steel and it's in two parts which are almost identical. The two parts are joined together with a screw which is kept fairly loose. Each of the parts has one round end and one pointed end. The difference between the two round ends is that one is large enough to put your thumb in and the other large enough to put two fingers in . . .

2 *Scrambled eggs*
  1 You need a non-stick saucepan, a small bowl, a wooden spoon, some eggs (2 per person), a little butter, a dash of milk, pepper and salt.
  2 Break the eggs into the bowl and add the pepper, salt and a dash of milk.
  3 Melt the butter in the saucepan and when it's hot, add the eggs.
  4 Stir constantly, mixing the eggs as they cook . . .

3 *Spanish omelette*
  1 Prepare some potatoes by peeling them and boiling them until they are just cooked. They must still be firm, not soft.
  2 Chop the potatoes into small cubes and put them on a warm plate. Keep the chopping board and knife.

3 Chop a large onion into small pieces and fry it in a frying pan in butter or olive oil until . . .

4 And an extra idea for written work: Write the instructions o how to do one of the processes, or operate one of the machi you described during this unit.

10 Talking about similarities, talking about differences, stating preferences

Functional objectives

Students will extend their ability to describe and discuss similarities and differences and to explain their preferences.

Presupposed knowledge

The use of common expressions describing quantity.
The use of the forms *more . . . than*, *as . . . as*, *many*, *much*, *a lot of*, *lots of*.
(*Notions in English* unit 41: Quantity; *English in Situations* A2, B2 and A5.)

10.1 Conversation

Alternatively, prepare a set of magazine advertisements for different cars – some quite similar, some very different. Talk with the class about the cars, pointing out similarities and differences. These advertisements can be pinned up in the classroom or for more permanent use stuck onto cards, so that they can be held up and passed around.

10.2 Presentation: talking about similarities

Demonstrate by using the recommended expressions as you state other similarities between the four countries – food, physical characteristics of the people, TV viewing habits, education systems etc.

To practise, ask each student to write down and report the similarities between his or her country and the four countries listed.

10.3 Practice in small groups

Monitor and correct mistakes. Ask for a report from each group afterwards.

10.4 Practice in pairs or small groups

A starting point might be to look at advertisements cut out from a magazine for different cars or other products. Get each group to compare them and report back to the class.

10.5 Presentation: talking about differences

Again, demonstrate by talking about other differences and ask each student to point out differences between his or her country and the UK or Ireland.

10.6 Practice in two large groups (a very large class may need more groups)

Make sure each group deals with the task as a businesslike 'committee'. Perhaps get each committee to compare their own country with the five countries listed.
Monitor each group and afterwards report to the class.

10.7 Practice in small groups

Monitor each group and report to the class on their performance.

10.8 Practice in small groups

Perhaps ask each group to 'specialize' in a different topic, so that the report they make to the rest of the class can be more detailed and interesting.

10.9 Practice in pairs

A starting point might be to remind the class what they talked about in unit 1 when they were 'Talking about themselves'. It might be worth referring back to 1.3.

10.10 Presentation: stating preferences

Ask for more ideas on how to state a preference:

I'd much rather . . .
It'd be best to . . .
The best one is . . .

To demonstrate and practise, either get a restaurant menu for the class to study and comment on, or with the class's help write a varied menu on the board and ask them to state their preferences.

10.11 Practice in groups of three or four

Perhaps suggest that each member of the groups tries to 'sell' a different place.

10.12 Practice in pairs

It may be necessary to begin by asking the class what they expect from a job – what pay, hours, type of work etc. Perhaps suggest that they are unemployed and *must* select one of the jobs.
(As additional written work they could 'apply in writing' for one of the jobs.)

10.13 Written work

Some possible openings:

1 Dear Sue,
As you're coming here next month, I'd like to tell you what to expect. To begin with the weather here is totally different from your weather – it hardly ever rains but

when it does, it rains very heavily. Another big difference is that . . .

2 *The Sun* and *The Daily Express*
Both these newspapers are morning papers and the immediate impression you get is that they are very similar in style and layout. Politically they are both on the right, though neither of them is a party newspaper. As far as their content is concerned, however, . . .

3 Discuss this topic with the class before they write. (No comment from me!)

11 Making suggestions and giving advice, expressing enthusiasm, persuading

Functional objectives

Students will extend their ability to help other people who are unsure what to do, to make enthusiastic suggestions, to persuade other people to accept their suggestions.

11.1 Conversation

Alternatively, tell the class that you are dissatisfied with your 'image' – the clothes you wear, your hair and general appearance. Get them to suggest how you could improve!

11.2 Presentation: making suggestions and giving advice

Note that it is the *content* of the advice which is more important than how you begin.
Ask for other ways to make suggestions:

How about . . . -ing . . .
One idea would be to . . .
I'd suggest that you . . .
Perhaps you ought to . . .

Get the class to make suggestions to a smoker on how to stop, using each of the expressions.

11.3 Practice as a class

Pretend that you are fed up with your job – ask the class to suggest what you should do. Tell them about your other problems too:
You are lonely
You find it hard to make friends
You are unfit

You don't know what to do this evening, this weekend and for your forthcoming holiday

Correct mistakes as you go along.

11.4 Practice in small groups

Perhaps begin by asking each student to make a list of his friends and relations back home (possibly inventing some of them). Monitor each group and report to the class.

11.5 Practice in groups

At the reporting-back stage, you could perhaps ask four students to pretend to be each of the letter-writers.

11.6 Communication activity in groups of four

Student A:	part one activity 43	part two activity 144
Student B:	part one activity 33	part two activity 126
Student C:	part one activity 83	part two activity 106
Student D:	part one activity 5	part two activity 64

(Student D can be left out to make one or two groups of three only.)

In part one each student is given a personal problem which he or she explains to the others and then asks for advice on. Each problem must be 'solved' before the next one is discussed. In part two there are four more problems.

Monitor each group (perhaps record one or two of the groups in action).

11.7 Presentation: expressing enthusiasm

Ask for other ideas:

How about this idea . . .
I know what we can do – let's . . .
I'll tell you what – why don't we . . .

Make sure the class uses the right *tone of voice*. Demonstrate and practise by talking about what to do this evening.

11.8 Practice in pairs and as a class

Perhaps start the ball rolling by enthusiastically suggesting:
a dictation next lesson!
a grammar test!!
a revision lesson!!!
etc.!!!!

After preparation in pairs, each pair reports to the rest of the class with enormous enthusiasm.

11.9 Communication activity in groups of three

Student A: activity 13
Student B: activity 119
Student C: activity 77
(An extra student can join A, B or C.)

Each 'friend' has his or her own plans for the weekend, which they must present enthusiastically to each other. A discussion follows and a compromise plan is to be agreed on.

At the end, ask each group to report on their compromise plans.

11.10 Presentation: persuading

Ask for other ideas on ways to raise objections:

That's alright in theory, but in practice . . .
You don't seem to realize that there's more involved . . .
You're living in a dream world!
I don't really think that would work because . . .

and other ways of answering objections:

Ah yes, but you didn't get the main point . . .
You're perfectly right, but don't you see that . . .

and perhaps suggest ways of giving in:

Oh yes, I hadn't realized that.

Oh no. My idea wouldn't work, would it?
Good Lord, I hadn't thought of that.

Practise by telling the class the details of your plan to climb Mount Everest. Then ask them to suggest their own plan.

11.11 Practice as a class

Begin by telling the class how much you smoke, drink and eat. Ask them to persuade you to cut down or stop. (You know it's all bad for you, but you enjoy smoking, drinking and over-eating.)

11.12 Communication activity in pairs

Student A: activity 141
Student B: activity 94
(An extra student can join A or B.)

Make sure each pair has time to study the activity page before they begin talking. A and B have agreed to go on holiday together. A has chosen a hotel in Austria, B a hotel in Tunisia. Each tries to persuade the other.

At the end, ask each pair what decision they reached.

11.13 Communication activity in groups of three or four

Student A: activity 72
Student B: activity 29
Student C: activity 4
Student D: activity 117 (can be omitted)

Make sure each student has time to study his or her advertisement before A begins. Each student has noticed a different advertisement in a magazine: A – a personal TV-radio; B – a quartz alarm clock; C – a digital watch; D – a handy bag. Each has to persuade the others that the purchase of his or her item is a fantastic idea.

Ask each group to report. Report to them on the monitoring you did.

11.14 Practice as a class or in groups

A chance for real problems to be solved – if necessary problems could be invented.

11.15 Written work

Some possible opening lines:

1 Dear Robert,

I'm very sorry to hear about your difficulty in concentrating on your exam revision. I know how important the exam is to you.

Have you ever thought of staying somewhere else before the exam? You could go to the country and . . .

2 Dear Richard,

In answer to your problem, yes I do have a few ideas. I suppose the best thing would be to have a party – not just the usual sort of party, but a party with surprises. One thing you could do is . . .

3 Dear Susan,

I was really very upset to hear about Mike. I'm sure he really will come back in a few days, after all it isn't the first time he's disappeared, is it? Really, the only thing to do is . . .

12 Complaining, apologizing and forgiving, expressing disappointment

Functional objectives

Students will extend their ability to point out politely that they are dissatisfied, to apologize for what they have done wrong, to break the news that they have an apology to make, to forgive other people and to express disappointment.

12.1 Conversation

Alternatively, enter the classroom looking upset. Break the news to the class that you have lost their homework, not prepared the lesson and have to leave early for a dental appointment. Ask them what they will say to your head of department or principal

12.2 Presentation: complaining

Ask for other ways to make a complaint:

There seems to be something wrong with . . .
I'm sorry to have to bring this up . . .

Point out that a direct complaint beginning, for example: '*Look here! . . .* ' is dangerous because it will antagonize people, perhaps even start an argument so that you won't get an apology or replacement of goods.

Practise with the class by asking them to imagine (a) what a teacher might do wrong and how they'd complain to a teacher who:
ignored some students
had a favourite student
spoke too fast
arrived late
didn't give back homework punctually
asked too many questions
didn't mark homework helpfully
set too much homework

and (b) how they might express dissatisfaction to a fellow-student who frequently:
arrives late
interrupts the lesson
doesn't do any homework
eats chewing gum in the lesson
doesn't listen to what you say to him or her

Correct mistakes and encourage a variety of suggestions.

12.3 Practice (pattern conversation)

Note the tactful use of *seem* in the conversation.
Monitor and perhaps make sure the 'guests' aren't being *too* polite!

12.4 Communication activity in two groups

Group A: part one (as shopkeepers) activity 60
part two (as customers) activity 90
Group B: part one (as customers) activity 6
part two (as shopkeepers) activity 27

In the first part, each student in group A sets up a shop (which sells everything) in a different area of the room. Then students from group B go from shop to shop complaining about the faulty goods on their list. In the second part, the roles are reversed.

Monitor and make sure each complaint is *politely* expressed.

12.5 Communication activity in pairs

Each student follows a rather long route through the communication activities so that each situation is fresh and there is no time for preparation:

Student A: activity 128 to 129 to 34 to 22 to 48 to 112
Student B: activity 54 to 65 to 116 to 138 to 137 to 89
(With an odd number of students, the extra one can be the husband or wife of A or B.)

First A has a complaint to make to B, then B to A and so on. It's best if each pair stands up, so that the participants can walk away from each other after each conversation and read what to do next before coming together again. The 'complainer' must be 'satisfied' each time before he or she goes away.
The complaints are about:

noisy children	(neighbours)
vicious dog	"
blocked drive	"
loud TV	"
meanness at the bar	(friends)
not inviting friend to party	"

Monitor appropriate language. If necessary, interrupt to make comments.

12.6 Presentation: apologizing and forgiving

Ask for other ways to apologize:

There's something I have to tell you . . .
You remember I promised to . . .

and other ways to forgive:

It's OK. It could happen to anyone.
It's nobody's fault really.

Practise by asking students what they would say to a friend whose dog has run away.
Then ask what a hotel receptionist might say to a guest if:
there is no hot water
dinner will not be served today
the room he reserved is not available
he has to move to a smaller room
he has to pay his bill in advance
he has been annoying other guests by singing in his bath
the air conditioning will be off all day

Ask students to suggest more hotel situations from their experience or imagination.

12.7 Practice (pattern conversation)

Perhaps do the conversations twice: once with A and B as good friends, then again as acquaintances. Or change roles half way. Monitor for appropriate language.

12.8 Communication activity in pairs

Student A: part one (as friend) activity 67 part two (as friend) activity 32 part three (as assistant) activity 134 part four (as boss) activity 120
Student B: part one (as friend) activity 36 part two (as friend) activity 14 part three (as boss) activity 95 part four (as assistant) activity 81
(An extra student can share A's roles.)

In each part, *both* students have an apology to make.

Monitor for appropriate language. Ask each pair to report to the rest of the class what happened.

12.9 Presentation: expressing disappointment

Demonstrate and practise by talking about how the bad weather (storm, snow, rain, hail, gale) has prevented you all from going on the picnic you planned (and the country walk and the bicycle ride and the trip to the beach).

12.10 Practice (pattern conversation)

Point out and practise the tones of voice used to show disappointment and when taking a disappointment philosophically. Correct mistakes in grammar or pronunciation.

12.11 Communication activity in groups of three

Student A: activity 148
Student B: activity 21
Student C: activity 62
(C can either be left out or two students can share C's role.)

Each student has some bad news to tell his or her friends whic he or she knows will disappoint them. They may need to be persuaded to take their setbacks philosophically.

Ask each group to report to the rest of the class what they did

12.12 Communication activity in pairs

Student A: part one (as student) activity 96
part two (as housewife) activity 146
Student B: part one (as housewife) activity 86
part two (as student) activity 26
(An extra student can share A's role and play 'another student and 'housewife's husband' or 'friend'.)

In each part the student has been left alone in the house while the lady of the house is out. The student has some bad news fo her on her return.

Monitor appropriate language and report to the class on their performance.

12.13 Written work

Some possible openings:

1 Dear Sirs,
Just over twelve months ago I bought an ACME radio-cassette player from your company. I have only used it occasionally and it has now gone wrong. The main fault seems to be that . . .

2 Dear Sirs,
I have just returned from a two-week holiday with your company in Malidorm. I am writing to you to complain about the hotel we stayed at, which was the Torre Defectiva. On our arrival at the hotel we were shocked to find that . . .

3 Dear Alan,
I really was very upset to hear about your exams. I know you worked very hard all through your course and really deserved to pass. I suppose it was a case of 'exam nerves' which we all suffer from but . . .

13 Describing places, describing people

Functional objectives

Students will extend their ability to describe the appearance of buildings, cities, towns and other kinds of places and their attitude to them, and to describe the appearance and character of people they know.

13.1 Conversation

Alternatively, describe to the class a place you know and someone who lives there, encouraging them to ask questions. Or describe your own house and the members of your family.

13.2 Presentation: describing places

To do this and the following practice section you really need a set of magazine (or calendar) pictures. These are best if pasted onto large cards so that they can be shown to the class and passed around.

Get the students to close their eyes for a moment and try to visualize the outside of the building you're in and the town you're in and the countryside around. Encourage them to try to describe each in as much detail as possible and to *ask* for the words they need. Here are just a few of the words they *might* need:

storey, facade, tiled roof, sloping roof, courtyard, drain-pipe, gutter . . .
shopping centre, pedestrian precinct, roundabout, narrow streets, broad avenues, office blocks . . .
woods, forests, agricultural land, estuary, mountain range, peak, snow-capped . . .

But this book cannot predict what they will need – only you and your students know that. So allow plenty of time for

questions at all stages of this unit. Write up the new and useful words and allow the students time to make notes.
Look together at some of your set of pictures, too.

13.3 Practice as a class

Spend some time encouraging questions about each postcard. Perhaps start the ball rolling by demonstrating how they might describe one of the scenes:

This is a beautiful little town beside a lake. In the distance there are high mountains, but you can't see them very clearly because there is a heat haze and visibility is poor. On the lake there's a steamer just arriving at . . .

Show the class more of your pictures and work out a good description of each.

You could also play the following *game* with your pictures or with smaller pictures pasted on postcards (perhaps cut out of holiday brochures): Divide the class into small groups, and give each student a card. The students should then describe their pictures without showing them to their partners. The others must try to visualize the scenes being described and they are allowed to ask questions, of course.

13.4 Practice in small groups

Perhaps demonstrate how to begin by describing a well-known building to the class and asking them to guess what it is (Empire State Building? Big Ben?).

13.5 Practice in groups of three or four

Again, you could give a glowing description of your favourite place first.
Monitor each group and report to the whole class.

13.6 Presentation: describing people

The ideal starting point for this is another set of magazine pictures, pasted onto large cards (in collecting these, look out for photos of people of different ages, in different moods and clothes – not just happy young fashion models). Alternatively, begin by looking at the people on the front cover of this book or thinking about absent friends or colleagues.

Encourage the class to *find out* the words they need from each other, from you, or from a dictionary. For example, they *might* need some of these words:

General personal impression: *likeable, aggressive, attractive, cheerful, he or she reminds me of . . . , looks like . . .*
Age: *thirtyish, in his or her early/mid-/late thirties, middle-aged, in his or her teens . . .*
Height*, weight*, build or figure: *tall and slim, athletic, well-built, over-weight . . .*
Face, hair, eyes, complexion: *oval face, curly hair, wavy hair, bushy eyebrows, Roman nose . . .*
Clothes: *well-dressed, casual clothes, baggy trousers, a loose jumper, cardigan . . .*
Character: *sensitive, bad-tempered, generous, narrow-minded, excitable, level-headed . . .*
Interests, sports and hobbies: *he's keen on sailing, she spends a lot of time knitting, sewing . . .*
Their life so far – achievements, family background etc.: *well-qualified, an only child, eldest daughter, single . . .*

(Make sure your students realize that it is extremely rude to say to someone something like this: 'You are a narrow-minded over-weight middle-aged person'!)

Spend plenty of time during this presentation stage *and* during the practice stages answering questions from the class for words they *need.*

*Note that most British and American people use feet and inches to describe height, and that the British often use stones to describe weight, while the Americans use pounds. For example:

6 foot = 1.83 metres	(1 foot = 12 inches)
5 foot 6 = 1.68 metres	(1 metre = 3 foot 3 inches
10 stone = 140 pounds = 63 kilos	(14 pounds = 1 stone)
12 stone = 168 pounds = 76 kilos	(1 kilo = 2.2 pounds)
15 stone = 210 pounds = 95 kilos	

13.7 Practice as a class

Perhaps use the picture cards again. Make sure each student describes *several* people.
Correct mistakes and supply needed words.

13.8 Practice as a class

Start the ball rolling by standing (or sitting) back-to-back with one student and describing him or her yourself. Then he or she describes you. Then let the first pair begin.
Supply needed words.

13.9 Practice in small groups

After the groups have finished, perhaps ask students to describe to the class:
their old school teacher
their boss
a local character
the school bully at their first school (or the child who was their 'best friend')
their landlady (if they are studying in Britain now)

13.10 Practice in groups of three or four

Monitor each group and report to the class afterwards. Ask each group to report their most vivid or interesting description to the class.

13.11 Written work

Some possible openings:

1 He's just over six foot tall and quite slim. He's got dark brown curly hair, which is quite long. He usually wears cord trousers or jeans with a matching pullover. He has brown eyes and a bent nose. He's clean shaven. He always wears a silver identity bracelet on his right wrist . . .

2 All the houses look the same in Alma Road. The one you want is about half-way down the road on the left. It has a natural wood front door with blue numbers on it. The front of the house is red-brick but if you look at the right-hand side you'll see that it's painted dark brown. There's a small tree just outside the front door and . . .

3 On the extreme left there's a man wearing a dark suit with a waistcoat and a striped tie. He looks a very conventional sort of person – he likes to do everything in the old-fashioned way. He's in his late fifties and . . .

. . . and an extra idea for written work:

4 Write a description of the most remarkable, *or* unpleasant, person you've ever met.
A possible opening:
Probably one of the most irritating people I know is about my age, but he looks quite a bit older. His main fault is that he never listens to what you say to him and is deaf to other people's ideas. He's also remarkably stupid, even though he pretends to be the great intellectual. Take the other day, for example . . .

14 Telling a story: narrative techniques, handling dialogue, controlling a narrative

Functional objectives

Students will extend their ability to sustain a narrative (as they tell the story of an interesting event or experience, an anecdote or the plot of a novel or film) by creating some suspense, involving the listener, using appropriate and closing phrases, marking digressions, giving full quotations or reporting the main points of what someone said.

Presupposed knowledge

Past forms of irregular verbs.
Methods of showing the sequence of events.
The use of past continuous and past perfect forms.
The rules of reported speech.
How to talk about past events, as practised in *Functions of English* unit 4.
(*Notions in English* unit 6: The past, unit 26: Reporting, unit 33: Sequence of events, and perhaps also unit 45: Dramatic inversion would be useful.)

14.1 Conversation

Alternatively, tell the class about an unforgettable experience of your own or an anecdote.

14.2 Presentation: narrative techniques

Perhaps use this story as a drill, getting students to rephrase each line using the *'what happened was'* and *'what he did was'* structures:

Crime doesn't pay?

John had a row with Bill.
Bill punched John on the nose.

John hit him back.
Bill fell out of the window.
And was killed.
John said to himself, 'Oh, my God!'
And started thinking what to do.
He looked around the room.
He saw Bill's wallet lying on the floor.
And he said, 'Good God!'
He picked it up.
And looked inside and found it was full of £20 notes.
He counted them.
He said, '50 notes, that makes £1,000.'
He put the money in his own wallet.
He went to a travel agent's.
And said, 'First class single to Nice, please.'
He went to the airport.
The plane took him to the French Riviera.
He went directly to the Casino in Monte Carlo.
He found a suitable roulette table.
He said, '£1,000 on number 7, please.'
Number 7 came up.
He thought, 'I'll try again.'
Number 7 came up again.
John had become a wealthy man.
He returned to the airport.
He bought a ticket to South America.
The plane got him there safely.
He bought a luxury apartment.
He said to himself, 'Poor old Bill.'
He opened another bottle of champagne.

Point out that such structures have to be used more sparingly in a real narrative!

Ask for more ways of involving the listener:

You may not believe this, but . . .
You may find this a bit hard to believe, but . . .

14.3 Practice as a class

Point out that the so-called 'historic' or 'narrative' present tense is often used in telling stories. It is often used in strip cartoons, to describe the plots of films or novels, and to tell anecdotes.

With the strip cartoon here, get the class to begin like this:

Last summer Jocasta and Belinda often used to go to the swimming pool on hot afternoons . . .

Correct mistakes and advise students how to tell the story in their own words – it may help to look at the story together first and then tell the story with books closed.

14.4 Communication activity in pairs

Student A: activity 135
Student B: activity 87
(An extra student can team up with A or B.)

Each student has a strip cartoon to put into his or her own words. Allow time for preparation.

Monitor and encourage students to add detail and dialogue, and to say what happened before and after.

14.5 Practice in groups

Possibly encourage the use of the present tense here:

. . . so Michael gets back from the war and his friends throw a party to welcome him home. But he feels embarrassed and goes to a motel that evening and arrives home just as the party is finishing . . .

Monitor and give advice.

14.6 Presentation: handling dialogue

Perhaps record an interview from the radio, or two students role-playing an interview, or yourself being interviewed. Use the recording as a starting point for practising reporting the main points (or gist) or the actual words.

14.7 Communication activity in pairs

Student A: activity 46
Student B: activity 111
(An extra student can team up with A or B.)

This activity is in three stages:

1 Each student has a short passage which is in reported speech. This passage has to be rewritten as a dialogue with the actual words of the speakers. This may need checking or correcting before the next stage.
2 Each student takes his or her partner's dialogue and rewrites it in reported form.
3 The rewritten reported text is compared with the original reported text in the partner's activity section.

Monitor and help out if students are having difficulty. Discuss the differences between the three versions.

14.8 Presentation: controlling a narrative

Use the strip cartoon from 14.3 again or a different strip cartoon you have cut out of a newspaper or magazine.

14.9 Communication activity in pairs

Student A: activity 140
Student B: activity 149
(An extra student can team up with B.)

Each student has a short anecdote to narrate to his or her partner. A has an adapted version of the James Thurber fable 'The Little Girl and the Wolf', B has a story about an ancient king. Make it clear to the students that they should try to 'spin the story out' by adding detail and dialogue. If they are listening they should ask the narrator questions as the story proceeds.

Monitor and report your comments to the class afterwards. How do they suggest their narrations could be improved?

14.10 Practice in small groups

Perhaps set the ball rolling by telling the class about an experience you have had – or a dream or anecdote.
Monitor each group and report on their performance at the end.

If your students seem confident enough, ask them all to prepare another story to tell the class in your next lesson. Something that once happened to them or to a friend or relation might be a suitable topic.

14.11 Practice as a class

In this game students should sit in a circle and every other student is called A while the person on his or her right is called B. If you have an odd number of students, you should join the circle yourself. The first round begins with each student A telling B a short experience, joke or funny story. This story is then told to the person on the right and so on round the circle until it returns to its source. The second round begins with all the B's telling another story to the A's on their right and so on round the circle. Between rounds ask everyone to report on how their story had changed by the time it got back to them.

14.12 Written work

Some possible openings:

1 Dear Caroline,
You'll never believe this but it really happened. I was sitting at home reading a book when the telephone rang. Well, I answered it and it was a voice I didn't recognize. The voice said . . .

2 ORDEAL OF HIJACK HOSTAGES
The 150 passengers held hostage in the Boeing 747 hijacked at Gatwick Airport were released last night unharmed. They had been held prisoner for 72 hours without food, drink or entertainment. The hijackers had threatened to . . .

and

We started our holiday three days later after a terrifying experience. Just as our plane was about to take off, an announcement came over the intercom to inform us that . . .

15 Dealing with moods and feelings: anger, sadness, indifference. Saying goodbye

Functional objectives

Students will extend their ability to deal with people who are angry, sad or indifferent, and to say goodbye in different ways.

15.1 Conversation

Alternatively, you could storm into the classroom slamming the door and pretend to be angry first, then become sad, then indifferent. Challenge your students to calm you down, cheer you up and arouse your interest. Or arrange for another teacher to come in 'unexpectedly', pretending to be angry about something. Calm him or her down and then say how depressed you are about something else. When you have been cheered up, pretend to be indifferent about something else. Then say goodbye to each other as if you're parting for ever.

15.2 Presentation: anger

This section focusses on interpreting degrees of anger and reacting to other people's anger. You may wish to change the focus by encouraging your students to get angry with each other; however it must be borne in mind that in real life they are unlikely to want to get angry with other people in English and that if they do, they will probably lose the ensuing argument with a native speaker.

Ask for ideas on other ways to express annoyance:

What a drag!
Oh dear, dear, dear!
Oh goodness!

Point out that the *tone of voice* may be the only sign that someone is annoyed (or is in a bad mood or furious). Demonstrate this.

Ask for ideas on other ways to express sarcasm:

That's absolutely marvellous!
It was very good!

And other swear words:

Shit!
Christ!
Bugger!

Point out that many people may be offended by 'bad language Students should avoid using swear words.

And other ways of being furious:

I can't stand the way he always . . .
This is the last straw . . .

The practice sections 15.3 and 15.4 concentrate on calming people who are angry. It might also be entertaining to spend a little time practising having arguments or provoking people int getting angry. Some surefire ways of antagonising someone are

Look here, you . . .
You stupid idiot!
Listen to me!
For God's sake, why don't you . . .
Don't be such a fool!

If your class agree that this kind of language might be worth practising, divide the students into two groups, for an extra communication activity which isn't referred to in the Student's Book. One group should look at activity 97 while the other looks at activity 131. Each group begins by discussing the most annoying behaviour of the other group. When they are ready they can start criticising each other. This can be done in pairs, small groups or in the original large groups. (The group looking at activity 97 are serious and humourless, the group looking at activity 131 are frivolous and lazy.)
Warning: if there are people in your class who dislike each other or who might get upset, don't do this communication activity!

15.3 Practice as a class

If students need extra ideas you could suggest an imaginary series of annoying things which have happened: a teacher lost their homework, they were late for school or work, their tea was too cold to drink, the weather is terrible, someone was rude to them, etc.
Perhaps tell the class how you hate waiting in queues and get them to calm you down.

15.4 Communication activity in pairs

Student A: activity 115 to 18 to 12 to 145 to 127 to 71
Student B: activity 42 to 130 to 118 to 113 to 88 to 76
(An extra student can join A or B.)

Each part of the activity has one student being angry and the other calming him or her down. The situations are being angry about:
an inconsiderate flat-mate called John
an unpunctual friend called John
an unsuccessful complaint in a shoe shop
being questioned by a store detective
being involved in a minor road accident
being cheated in a restaurant (which the friend is thought to have recommended, but in fact didn't).

15.5 Presentation: sadness

Demonstrate and practise by telling the class some of your own imaginary problems and getting them to cheer you up:
Your wife/husband has just left you
Your children are ill
Your grandmother has died
You've lost your watch
You've had a row with your best friend
etc.

15.6 Communication activity in pairs

Student A: part one activity 103 part two activity 152
Student B: part one activity 59 part two activity 66
(An extra student can team up with A or B.)

First, student B has a list of disasters which have befallen him o her and student A has to cheer B up. Then, when B is happier, A is depressed and has to be cheered up.

Monitor and offer sympathetic advice.

15.7 Communication activity in pairs

Student A: activity 121 to 37 to 24 to 139 to 125
Student B: activity 49 to 28 to 68 to 78 to 15

In each part of the activity one student has a problem and the other must try to cheer him or her up. The sad partner must be cheered up before the pair can look at the next activity.

15.8 Presentation: indifference

Perhaps demonstrate and practise by telling the students how indifferent you are to hearing about their various jobs or hobbies. Get them to arouse your interest.

Point out and demonstrate that indifference is often only expressed by tone of voice:

Oh, yeah?
I see.
Very nice.
Interesting.

15.9 Communication activity in pairs

Student A: part one activity 153 part two activity 147
Student B: part one activity 55 part two activity 122
(An extra student can join A or B.)

A begins by being indifferent to B's ideas, and then B pretends to be indifferent to A's ideas.

15.10 Practice as a class

Begin by dividing the class into four groups: group A to be in a bad temper, group B depressed, group C indifferent and group D in a good mood. After each group has got together and established its mood, get everyone to stand up and talk to different people from other groups trying to influence them to share their mood. At the end, find out what happened. Were they able to change anyone else's mood?

15.11 Presentation: saying goodbye

Ask for other ideas on saying goodbye informally when you are meeting again soon:

See you later!
See you soon!
Bye now!

(Perhaps point out that 'Byebye' sometimes sounds a little childish and that in a more formal situation you can say: *Goodbye!* or *Good night!* – at the end of the day's work.)

Ask for other ideas on saying goodbye for ever or for a long time:

I hope everything goes well.
Well . . .
Let's hope it's au revoir.

15.12 Practice as a class

Everyone has to say goodbye to everyone else in the room, pretending that this is their last meeting.

15.13 Communication activity

Everyone looks at activity 45, which says goodbye to them.

15.14 Written work

Begin by discussing the topic – the class's comments will be useful for you the next time you use *Functions of English.*

Recorded Exercises tapescript

Introduction

The cassettes for the *Functions of English* Recorded Exercises can be used by students in a language laboratory, or without a teacher in a private-study laboratory or on their own with a normal cassette recorder. To use the cassettes, students need the accompanying workbook, which contains the examples of all the exercises and the necessary prompts, together with pictures, diagrams and communication activities.

Each set of exercises is directly related to the equivalent unit in *Functions of English*. It is probably best not to do the exercises until at least part of a unit has been covered in class. The exercises stimulate production of selected expressions presented in *Functions of English*.

Using the exercises in a language laboratory

If possible, try to *pre-record* the complete set of exercises for a unit (with all the exercises on the same side of the cassette) before the class arrive in the laboratory, so that they will be able to work at their own speed through the exercises. Your role during the laboratory lesson is to monitor, answer questions and offer advice. Make sure your students realize that they are responsible for their own work and that you are not watching over them like a worried parent. This feeling of student responsibility for their own work is essential because of the nature of many of the exercises, which are much more open-ended than conventional language laboratory drills. Even when model answers are given in the three-phase exercises, these are not the best possible 'correct' answers, which students are expected to aspire to – they are simply *suggested* appropriate answers; different responses are likely to be just as appropriate or even more appropriate. Your students should be developing their ability to *judge for themselves* the appropriacy (and accuracy) of what they have said. They may need some help at first, but you will find that this ability soon develops with a little encouragement.

The communication activity in each unit is not recorded on the tape but is printed in the workbook. Students will need to work in pairs for the communication activities. If your language laboratory has a 'double-plugging' facility, which enables two students to be plugged into the same booth and record both voices, you have the ideal set-up. Alternatively, two students sitting close together talking into the same microphone and listening later through different earphones of the same headset will also work. On the other hand, you may not always want the students to record themselves in this activity, which means that it can be done in the classroom as a follow up to the laboratory lesson.

Students working alone

In a private-study laboratory (a free-study language laboratory with recording facility, but no teacher), the same procedure would be followed as in a language laboratory. However, if students wish to use the cassettes on their own with a normal cassette recorder, they won't be able to record their responses unless they follow the procedure outlined below. In spite of this, they will still be getting valuable speaking practice and consolidating what they have done in class. Most students find that this kind of exercise, where the speed of the tape imposes a 'pressure' on them, is extremely useful.

Students *can* record their responses if a second cassette recorder is available: with the master cassette in cassette recorder 1 on *play* and a blank cassette in cassette recorder 2 on *record*, it is possible to go through each exercise recording one's own voice together with the master recording. Later one can listen to the final recording on cassette recorder 2 and if necessary repeat the drill by rewinding both cassettes. This procedure may sound a bit complicated at first, but after a few goes the routine is easy to follow.

The tapescript

If you are using the Recorded Exercises in a language laboratory the tapescript will help you to get an overall view of each unit. The instructions on the tape will normally be enough for students to follow, but less advanced students may need some extra explanation. The pauses on the tape where students are expected to speak are shown in the tapescript like this: ....

Unit 1 Talking about yourself, starting a conversation, making a date

Cassette 1
Side 1

Hallo. You are listening to the first of a series of fifteen units of extra practice material to accompany *Functions of English*. These tapes can be used with your teacher in a language laboratory or on your own.

Please look at unit 1 in your workbook. As you can see, the workbook gives two examples of each of the exercises. Some of these exercises require you to follow a pattern and some of the exercises are more open-ended and require you to answer truthfully from your own experience.

Exercise 1 Answering questions about yourself

Please look at the examples for exercise 1. The bold print shows you your part in each brief conversation. Now, listen carefully, please:

Woman: Hello, what's your name?
Model: My name's Leo Jones – do call me Leo.
Woman: Where do you come from?
Model: I come from Bournemouth – that's in the south of England, on the coast.

Now reply to these questions about yourself. After you have spoken you will hear a model answer – don't worry if this is different from your own answer – it's there for comparison with your answer later when you listen to the tape again afterwards.

Woman: Hello. What's your name? [pause for student response:] ....
Model: My name's Leo Jones – do call me Leo.
Woman: Where do you come from? ....
Model: I come from Bournemouth – that's in the south of England, on the coast.
Woman: Where were you born? ....
Model: I was born near Liverpool, but I was brought up in Ipswich.
Woman: What do you do? ....
Model: I'm a teacher – I teach English to foreign students.
Woman: Where are you living at the moment? ....
Model: I'm living at 108 Alma Road in Winton.
Woman: Do you know Britain very well? ....

Model: Well, I know the south of England quite well, but I've only spent a short time in the north.
Woman: Have you ever been to the United States? ....
Model: No I haven't, but I've been to Canada.
Woman: What are your plans for the next few weeks? For example, do you plan to do any travelling? ....
Model: I might go away for a weekend somewhere, but I'm going to be pretty busy for the rest of this month otherwise.
Woman: Thank you very much. ....
Model: My pleasure.

Now you should either listen to the conversation again *or* work through it again *or* go on to the next exercise and come back to this exercise later on.

Before we start the next exercise, we'd like you to comment on these sentences. Listen carefully:

(rising intonation) Man: It's a lovely day, isn't it. ↑

What was wrong with that? ....
Yes, the intonation was wrong, wasn't it?
And how about this?

(pause) Man: It's a lovely day . . . isn't it. ↓

What was wrong with that? ....
Yes, there was a pause in the middle, wasn't there?
And how about this?

(aggressive) Man: It's a lovely day, isn't it.

What was wrong with that? ....
Yes, the tone of voice was wrong, wasn't it?
And finally this one.

(correct) Woman: It's a lovely day, isn't it. ↓

Anything wrong with that? ....
No, that was quite alright, wasn't it?

Exercise 2 Starting a conversation

In this exercise you'll be starting conversations with people. Look at the examples in your workbook. Remember that the bold print shows you what you have to say. Listen very carefully to the *tone of voice* the speakers use in the examples:

Presenter: Picture one
Model: What a nice day, isn't it?
Stranger: Yes, it certainly is. It's lovely.
Model: It makes a nice change from yesterday.
Stranger: Mmm, yes.

Presenter: Picture two
Model: Not very nice weather, is it?
Stranger: No, it's awful.
Model: Still, let's hope it gets better before the weekend!
Stranger: Mmm, let's hope so.

Now imagine you're talking to a stranger at the bus stop. Comment on the weather in each of the pictures and respond to the stranger optimistically! Don't worry if the model sentences are slightly different from what you say.

Presenter: Picture one ....
Model: What a nice day, isn't it?
Stranger: Yes, it certainly is. It's lovely. ....
Model: It makes a nice change from yesterday.
Stranger: Mmm, yes.

Presenter: Picture two ....
Model: Not very nice weather, is it?
Stranger: No, it's dreadful. ....
Model: Still, let's hope it gets better before the weekend!
Stranger: Mmm, let's hope so.

Presenter: Picture three ....
Model: It's nice and warm today, isn't it?
Stranger: Mmm, I think we're in for a spell of fine weather. ....
Model: Yes, let's hope it lasts for the weekend.
Stranger: Oh, I think it will.

Presenter: Picture four ....
Model: It's very cold for July, isn't it?
Stranger: Yes, it's freezing. ....
Model: Let's hope it gets warmer soon.
Stranger: Mmm, it ought to be much warmer at this time of year.

Presenter: Picture five ....
Model: It's very warm today, isn't it?
Stranger: A bit too warm for my liking, I must say. ....
Model: Still, it's better than being too cold.
Stranger: Well, I'm not so sure, I can't stand the heat myself.

Presenter: Picture six ....
Model: This snow is lovely, isn't it?
Stranger: Well yes, but it means all the buses will be late. ....
Model: Still, I don't think it'll last long.
Stranger: Let's hope not.

Fine! When you go through the exercise again, pay particular attention to your *tone of voice*. Compare your answers carefully with the model answers. That's the end of exercise 2.

Exercise 3 Inviting someone out

In this exercise you'll be practising inviting different people out. Look at the examples in your workbook and listen very carefully to how these speakers express politeness by their tone of voice:

Presenter: Here's Bill.
Model: Hallo, Bill, have you got any plans for this evening?
Bill: Not really, no.
Model: Well, would you like to have a meal with me?
Bill: Oh, well, I'm not sure I can manage that.
Model: There's a nice Chinese restaurant in town – the food's very good there.
Bill: Oh, that sounds very nice, thanks.
Model: I'll call for you about 8, then.
Bill: 8 o'clock. Fine, thanks.

Presenter: Here comes Sue.
Model: Hallo, Sue, have you got any plans for tomorrow evening?
Sue: No, I don't think so. Um, no, I'm free.
Model: Well, I was wondering if you'd like to come to the cinema with me.
Sue: Oh, what are you going to see?
Model: There's this new American thriller on – it's supposed to be very exciting.
Sue: Oh, I'm not too keen on thrillers, so I'd rather not if you don't mind.
Model: Oh, what a pity. Still, perhaps some other time, then?
Sue: Sure – I like romantic films best.

Now it's your turn. Follow the pattern and speak during the pauses. Use the prompts in your workbook. Imagine you're talking to friends.

Presenter: Here's Bill. ....
Model: Hallo, Bill, have you got any plans for this evening?
Bill: Not really, no. ....
Model: Well, would you like to have a meal with me then?
Bill: Oh, well, I'm not sure I can manage that. ....
Model: There's a nice Chinese restaurant in town – the food's very good there.
Bill: Oh, that sounds very nice, yes. ....
Model: I'll call for you about 8, then.
Bill: 8 o'clock. Fine, thanks.

Presenter: Here comes Sue. ....
Model: Hallo, Sue, have you got any plans for tomorrow evening?
Sue: No, I don't think so. Um, no, I'm free. ....
Model: Well, I was wondering if you'd like to come to the cinema with me.
Sue: Oh, what's on? ....
Model: There's a new American thriller on – it's supposed to be very exciting.
Sue: Oh, I'm not too keen on thrillers, so I'd rather not if you don't mind. ....
Model: Oh, what a pity. Still, perhaps some other time, then?
Sue: Sure – I like romantic films best, by the way.

Presenter: It's Jane, look. ....
Model: Hallo, Jane, have you got any plans for next weekend?
Jane: Next weekend? No, I haven't got anything on. ....
Model: Well, I was wondering if you'd like to come to London with me?
Jane: London? Not really – I've seen quite a lot of London recently. ....
Model: Oh, well I was thinking of seeing the sights and having a nice meal somewhere.
Jane: It sounds a nice idea, but I'd rather not if you don't mind. ....
Model: Oh, what a pity. Still, perhaps some other time, then.
Jane: Yes, perhaps when the weather improves. Oh, and thanks anyway.

Presenter: Here's Bob. ....
Model: Hallo, Bob, have you got any plans for Friday evening?
Bob: Well, I was thinking of going to the pub on Friday. ....

Model: Oh, well I was wondering if you'd like to spend the evening studying with me.
Bob: Studying? On Friday night? ....
Model: Yes, we could go over our notes and test each other on vocabulary.
Bob: Well, it's a sensible idea, but I'd rather not work on Friday evening. ....
Model: Oh, what a pity. Still, perhaps some other time, then.
Bob: Yes, perhaps Monday. That'd suit me better.

Presenter: Look, it's Anne. ....
Model: Hallo, Anne, have you got any plans for Saturday?
Anne: Saturday? No, I was going to go to London but the trip's been called off. ....
Model: Well, would you like to come for a drive in the country with me?
Anne: That sounds nice. Where are you planning to go? ....
Model: I was thinking of driving to a pub for lunch and then having a look at the countryside.
Anne: What a lovely idea. Thanks for inviting me. ....
Model: I'll pick you up about 11, then.
Anne: 11 o'clock? Fine, I'll be ready.

That's the end of exercise 3. Don't forget to check your tone of voice when you go through this exercise again.

Exercise 4 Reacting to the unexpected

This exercise is quite unlike the previous ones – what you say depends on how you feel and how you react to the voices you hear. All you have to do is to reply to the remarks in a natural way. Here's an example:

Stranger 1: This bloody weather!
Model: Yes, it's awful, isn't it?
or: Oh, I don't know, I quite like it myself.

The model answers are for guidance only, so don't let them put you off! Ready?

Stranger 1: This bloody weather! ....
Model: I know, it's dreadful, isn't it?

Stranger 2: So you come from Switzerland, do you? ....
Model: No, I don't actually. I'm Austrian.

Stranger 1: You speak English very well, you know. ....
Model: Oh, do you think so? Thanks very much.

Stranger 2: It's the first time I've ever met someone from your country. ....
Model: Oh, I find that hard to believe, there are lots of us here.

Stranger 1: I've been to your country on holiday. It was horrible! ....
Model: Oh, you can't really tell what a country's like from a short visit, you know.

Stranger 2: How old did you say you were? ....
Model: I'm 28.
Stranger 2: Sorry, I didn't catch what you said. ....
Model: I said I was 28.
Stranger 2: Oh, I'd have said you were five years younger than that. ....
Model: Oh, thank you, people often say I don't look my age.

Stranger 1: Look, your English is almost perfect, so what on earth are you learning English for? ....
Model: Oh, it's not as good as all that. I've still got a lot to learn, you know.

Stranger 2: Well, I must be off. Nice meeting you. ....
Model: Nice meeting *you*. Goodbye.

That's the end of exercise 4.
There's a communication activity for you to do with a partner. Please look at your workbook for the instructions. If you're working in a language laboratory, call your teacher when you're ready for this.
That's the end of unit 1. Please rewind your tape to the beginning.

Arrange the class into pairs for the communication activity. One member of each pair should look at activity C, while his or her partner looks at activity M. Students have to make contact with each other (they are 'strangers'), ask and answer questions and arrange another meeting.
In a language laboratory, don't use the Recorded Exercises tape but record silence on the master track while the students record onto the student track. Allow time for the students to listen through their recording at the end.

Unit 2 Asking for information: question techniques, answering techniques, getting more information

In this second unit we're concentrating on getting and giving information. Look at unit 2 in your workbook.

Exercise 1 Asking for information

Listen carefully to the examples:

Presenter: One
Model: Excuse me.
Stranger: Yes?
Model: I was wondering if you could help me. I'd like to know when the last train to London leaves.
Stranger: I think there's one at 11.46, but you'd better check at the station.
Model: I see, thanks very much.

Presenter: Two
Model: Excuse me.
Stranger: Yes?
Model: I wonder if you could tell me what time the last bus to town leaves.
Stranger: Well, I'm not sure, but I think it leaves here at about 11.
Model: I see, thanks very much.

Now find out the remaining information in your workbook. Start again at number one. Imagine you're asking someone who can probably answer your questions. Make a note of each answer.

Presenter: One ....
Model: Excuse me.
Stranger: Yes? ....
Model: I was wondering if you could help me. I'd like to know when the last train to London leaves.
Stranger: Yes, it leaves at 11.46. ....
Model: I see, thank you very much.

Presenter: Two ....
Model: Excuse me.
Stranger: Yes? ....
Model: I wonder if you could tell me what time the last bus to town leaves.

Stranger: Well, I'm not entirely sure, but I think it leaves here at about 11. ....
Model: I see, thanks very much.

Presenter: Three ....
Model: Excuse me.
Stranger: Yes? ....
Model: I wonder if you could help me. I'd like to know what time the pubs open on Sundays.
Stranger: Well, at lunchtime they open from 12 to 2 and in the evening they open at 7. ....
Model: I see, thanks very much.

Presenter: Four ....
Model: Excuse me.
Stranger: Yes? Can I help you? ....
Model: I wonder if you could tell me what evening the programme at the cinema changes.
Stranger: Yes, it usually changes on Thursdays. You can find out the programme if you get a local paper. ....
Model: I see, thank you very much.

Presenter: Five ....
Model: Excuse me.
Stranger: Mmm? ....
Model: I was wondering if you could help me. Do you happen to know if there's a chemist open late this evening?
Stranger: Let me think . . . yes, there's one in the High Street. It's called Jackson and Jameson. ....
Model: I'm sorry, I didn't quite catch the name.
Stranger: Oh sorry, yes Jackson and Jameson. OK? ....
Model: I see, thank you very much.

End of exercise 1.

Exercise 2 Asking for information

Look at your workbook and listen to the beginning of this conversation.

Model: Good morning.
Info. officer: Good morning, can I help you?
Model: Yes, I'd like to know something about the weather in Bournemouth.
Info. officer: Well, it's fairly mild – warm but not too hot in the summer and it's one of the driest places in Britain.

Model: I see, could you tell me what the weather's like i
the autumn?
Info. officer: Well, in September you can expect ...... [*fade*]

Now imagine you are asking an information officer on the Bournemouth publicity coach about Bournemouth. Make note of the answers in your workbook. Start again at the beginning of the conversation by saying 'Good morning!' Ready? Start now.

....

Model: Good morning.
Info. officer: Good morning, can I help you? ....
Model: Yes, I'd like to know something about the weath
in Bournemouth.
Info. officer: Well, it's fairly mild – warm but not too hot in summer and there's less rain than elsewhere in Britain. ....
Model: I see, could you tell me what the weather's like i
autumn?
Info. officer: Well, in September and October you can expect sunny days and not too much rain, but the evenings tend to be quite cool. ....
Model: I see, I wonder if you could tell me something about the evening entertainments?
Info. officer: Yes, there are several cinemas, stage shows in the summer, night clubs and discos – and of course plenty of pubs and restaurants. ....
Model: I see, could you tell me a bit more about the stag
shows?
Info. officer: Well, they're mostly variety shows for British summer visitors – I don't think they're really ver
suitable for foreign visitors. ....
Model: I see, could you tell me a bit more about the restaurants?
Info. officer: Yes, there are Italian, Indian, Chinese, Middle Eastern, Greek restaurants – there's even a Swiss restaurant, believe it or not! ....
Model: I see, but could you tell me if there are any typically English restaurants?
Info. officer: That's a bit more difficult. To get a good English meal you need to eat in one of the hotels or with an English family. ....
Model: I see, could you tell me something about accommodation in Bournemouth?

Info. officer: Yes, you have a choice of staying in a hotel – from a five-star luxury hotel down to a simple bed-and-breakfast place – or renting a holiday flat – or if you go to a language school, staying with an English family. ....

Model: I see, could you tell me a bit more about bed-and-breakfast places?

Info. officer: For a few nights that's probably the best – they only provide you with a room and breakfast in the morning, so it works out cheaper and you're more independent in the evening as far as meals are concerned. ....

Model: I see, something else I'd like to know is this: are there any sports facilities?

Info. officer: Oh yes, plenty. You can play tennis, go sailing, play squash, play golf – you can even learn to windsurf. ....

Model: I see, could you tell me a bit more about windsurfing?

Info. officer: Mmm, yes. I do quite a lot of it myself – it's fantastic. You know, you stand on a board, holding the sail and the wind carries you along. It's amazingly easy to learn, too – though you get a bit wet at first! ....

Model: I see, well thanks very much for your help.

Info. officer: Don't mention it – I hope you'll come to Bournemouth soon! ....

Model: Yes, it sounds very nice, I'd like to!

That's the end of exercise 2.

Exercise 3 Asking for more information

Imagine you're working temporarily in an English office. You've just arrived on your first day and you want a colleague to tell you some things about the office routine and the other people in the office. Listen to the beginning of the conversation first.

Model: Excuse me, I'm new here. My name's Peter. Peter Grey.

Colleague: Pleased to meet you. I'm Mary. Mary Green.

Model: Hallo. Sorry to bother you, but could you give me some information about the office?

Colleague: Certainly, yes. What would you like to know?

Model: Well, first of all, I'd like to know where I can get a cup of coffee.
Colleague: Yes, there's a .... [*fade*]

Now look at the notes in your workbook and ask your colleag for the information you want. Make a note of the answers. Sta by explaining who you are.

....

Model: Excuse me, I've started here today. My name's Pete Peter Grey.
Colleague: Hallo. I'm Mary Green. ....
Model: Hallo. Sorry to bother you, but I'd like to know some things about the office.
Colleague: Mmm, yes. What would you like to know? ....
Model: Well, first of all, I'd like to know where I can get a cup of coffee.
Colleague: Yes, there's a coffee machine on the next floor up, but it's not very nice. If you can wait till 11, when the canteen opens, you can get quite reasonable coffee there. ....
Model: I'd also like to know if you're allowed to receive personal calls in the office.
Colleague: Well, no, actually. Mr Brown is quite strict about that. Unless it's an emergency, of course. ....
Model: Something else I'd like to know is this: what's the name of Mr Brown's secretary?
Colleague: She's called Susan, but she prefers to be called Miss Black. ....
Model: This may seem a stupid question, but what's Mr Brown like?
Colleague: Oh, he's alright. I know he *seems* very strict and unfriendly, but when you get to know him he's very sweet. ....
Model: Something else I'd like to know is this: what's the busiest time of day here?
Colleague: Well, usually there's not much to do before about 10. Oh, and we normally get a rush of work about a hour before lunch. Then it never stops till going-home time. ....
Model: I see. I need to go to the bank at lunchtime, can you tell me where the nearest one is?
Colleague: Well, there are two opposite each other just round the corner. You turn left outside the office and it's a few minutes' walk. ....

Model: OK fine. There's just one more thing I'd like to know. Can you tell me if there's somewhere you can recommend where I can have lunch?

Colleague: Yes, there's a nice little snack bar near the banks. I'm going off for lunch there at 1 o'clock. Perhaps you'd like to join me? ....

Model: That'd be lovely. Thanks very much for all your help.

Colleagie: Not at all. If there's anything else you'd like to know, all you have to do is ask. ....

Model: OK. Thanks again!

That's the end of exercise 3.

Exercise 4 Giving information

Imagine you're still working in the office you found out about in exercise 3. This time a new member of staff is asking *you* for information. Listen to the beginning of the conversation first.

New colleague: Excuse me. I'm new here.

Model: Oh, hallo. My name's Peter Grey.

New colleague: I'm Janet White. Can you tell me something about the work here?

Model: Of course, yes. What would you like to know?

New colleague: Well, first of all . . .

Now, using the notes you made in exercise 3, answer Janet's questions. Ready? There are no model answers given in this exercise.

New colleague: Excuse me. Can you help me? I'm new here. ....

New colleague: I'm Janet, Janet White. Can you tell me some things about the work here? ....

New colleague: Well, I'm dying for a cup of coffee. Where can I get one? ....

New colleague: And I gave my boyfriend the office telephone number. Is that OK? I mean, are we allowed to take personal calls? ....

New colleague: I've only met Mr Brown once – he seemed horrible. What's he like when you get to know him? ....

New colleague: Ah, I see. And his secretary, Miss Black. What's her first name? ....

New colleague: There doesn't seem much work to do at the moment. Is it always like this? ....

New colleague: Something else I'd like to know is this: is the a bank handy? I need to cash a cheque. ....

New colleague: Oh, and one last thing: can you recommend somewhere for lunch? Not too expensive, of course. ....

New colleague: Great! And thanks ever so much for all your help. ....

That's the end of exercise 4.

Exercise 5 Reacting to the unexpected

In this exercise you'll hear several different people. React appropriately to each person. Here's an example:

Man 1: I don't know anything about politics.
Model: Oh, no, neither do I really.

Now listen carefully and reply. The model answers are for guidance only.

Man 1: I don't know anything about politics. ....
Model: Oh, no, neither do I really.

Woman: I've spent ten years studying linguistics. ....
Model: Ten years? That's a very long time.

Man 2: What do you know about the Prime Minister? ....
Model: Not much, I'm not even sure what the PrimeMiniste name is!

Man 1: How do you spell 'technique'? ....
Model: I think it's TECHNIQUE.

Woman: Is the right word 'appropriateness' or 'appropriacy'? ....
Model: I think they're both English words, but 'appropriateness' is the one I've heard most used.

Man 1: Good God! You don't know much do you! ....
Model: Oh well, I think everybody's got *some* gaps in their knowledge.

Man 2: Glasgow *is* the capital of Scotland, isn't it? ....
Model: No, actually it's Edinburgh. Glasgow's the largest city though.

Woman: Which is the best restaurant in town? ....
Model: That's a very good question – it all depends what sort of food you prefer.

Man 2: What's the difference in meaning between someone and somebody? ....
Model: I don't think there is any difference. They mean the same thing.

That's the end of exercise 5.
There's a communication activity for you to do with a partner, next. For the instructions on what to do, look at your workbook. If you're working in a language laboratory, call your teacher when you're ready for this.
End of unit 2. Please rewind your tape now.

The communication activity is in two parts: in part one one student is the assistant in an electrical shop (giving information about radio-cassette recorders) while his or her partner is a customer on the telephone; in part two one student wants to go on a coach excursion, while his or her partner is in the coach station information office (giving details of the week's tour programme). One student looks at activity T, while the other looks at activity L. The activity practises asking for and giving information.

Unit 3 Getting people to do things: requesting, attracting attention, agreeing and refusing

Hallo. In this unit we are going to practise ways of asking people to do things. Remember that a polite tone of voice is essential. Look at unit 3 in your workbook.

Exercise 1 Asking a friend to do something

Listen to these examples. The two people talking are friends.

Presenter: One
Model: Do you think you could give me a sheet of writing paper?
Friend: Writing paper? Let's see if I've got any – yes, here you are.
Model: Thanks very much.

Presenter: Two
Model: I wonder if you could lend me a pen?
Friend: A pen? Well, here's a *red* ball-point, is that OK?
Model: Yes, fine, thanks very much.

Now, start again and ask for the things on your list. Imagine you're talking to a friend.

Presenter: One ....
Model: Do you think you could give me a sheet of writing paper?
Friend: Writing paper? Let's see if I've got any – oh yes, here you are. ....
Model: Thanks very much.

Presenter: Two ....
Model: I wonder if you could lend me a pen?
Friend: A pen? Well, here's a *red* ball-point, is that OK? ....
Model: Yes, fine, thanks very much.

Presenter: Three ....
Model: You couldn't lend me a dictionary for a moment, could you?
Friend: A dictionary? What do you need a dictionary for? ....
Model: To check my spelling, actually.
Friend: I see, yes, here you are, then. ....
Model: Thanks very much.

Presenter: Four ....
Model: Do you think you could lend me an envelope?
Friend: I've only got these *brown* ones. ....
Model: Oh, one of those'll do fine, thanks very much.

Presenter: Five ....
Model: I wonder if you could give me a stamp?
Friend: I think I've got some . . . Yes, here you are. It *is* for a letter abroad, isn't it? ....
Model: Yes, that's right, thanks ever so much.

Presenter: Six ....
Model: I'm very sorry, but I've forgotten Tom's address in Paris. You couldn't tell me it could you?
Friend: I suppose so. Yes, here it is in my address book, look! ....
Model: Fine, that's all I need. Thanks very much.
Friend: That's alright.

Remember to check your fluency and pronunciation.
End of exercise 1.

Exercise 2 Asking a stranger to do something

You need things to write a letter with again, but you're asking someone you don't know very well – so you need to be more polite. Listen to these examples:

Presenter: One
Model: I'm sorry to trouble you, but I wonder if you could possibly give me a sheet of writing paper.
Stranger: Certainly, yes. Here you are.
Model: Oh, thank you very much.

Presenter: Two
Model: Um, I wonder if you could possibly lend me a pen. Mine doesn't seem to work.
Stranger: Oh yes, here you are, mine works alright.
Model: Thank you very much indeed.

Now let's start again. Imagine you're talking to someone you don't know very well.

Presenter: One ……
Model: I'm sorry to trouble you, but I wonder if you could possibly give me a sheet of writing paper.
Stranger: Certainly, yes. Here you are. ……
Model: Oh, thank you very much.

Presenter: Two ……
Model: Um, I wonder if you could possibly lend me a pen. Mine doesn't seem to work.
Stranger: Certainly, yes, use mine! ……
Model: Thank you very much indeed.

Presenter: Three ……
Model: Sorry to trouble you again, but I wonder if you could possibly lend me your dictionary.
Stranger: Certainly, yes, but it's an English-to-English dictionary. ……
Model: That's alright, I just want to check my spelling.
Stranger: Here you are then. ……
Model: Thank you very much indeed.

Presenter: Four ....
Model: I'm ever so sorry to disturb you again, but I wonder if you could possibly give me an envelope.
Stranger: An envelope, no I'm sorry. I haven't got one. ....
Model: Oh dear, well never mind. Thanks anyway.

Presenter: Five ....
Model: Excuse me again, but I wonder if you could possib tell me where I could buy some envelopes?
Stranger: Mmm. Yes, there's a newsagent's on the corner. They sell stationery. ....
Model: Oh good. Thank you very much indeed.

Presenter: Six ....
Model: Um, sorry to trouble you again, but could you possibly give me change for £5?
Stranger: £5? Let me see – no, I'm afraid I've only got £4 o me. ....
Model: Oh dear, well never mind. I'll try at the newsagent' then. Thanks anyway.
Stranger: That's alright. Goodbye. ....
Model: Goodbye and thanks very much for all your help.

That's the end of exercise 2.

Exercise 3 Asking your employees to do something

Look at your workbook and listen to these examples: the manager is talking to some of her employees on the internal phone.

Brown: John Brown here.
Model: Hallo, Mr Brown. Have you got a moment?
Brown: Yes, Ms Green, of course.
Model: Well, I'd like you to cancel my appointment with Mr Black tomorrow afternoon.
Brown: Certainly, shall I tell him why?
Model: Yes, just tell him I've got an important board meetin he'll understand.
Brown: Fine, I'll do that right away.
Model: Thank you.

White: Hallo. Peter White speaking.
Model: Hallo Mr White. Have you got a moment?
White: Yes, Ms Green, certainly.

Model: Well, I'd like you to phone Mr Grey and arrange an appointment for tomorrow lunchtime.
White: Certainly, shall I tell him what it's about?
Model: Yes, just tell him it's very important for both of us, he'll understand.
White: Fine, I'll get on to him right away.
Model: Thanks.

Now start again, following the same pattern. You are Ms Green, the manager.

Brown: John Brown here. ....
Model: Hallo, Mr Brown. Have you got a moment?
Brown: Yes, Ms Green, of course. ....
Model: Well, I'd like you to cancel my appointment with Mr Black tomorrow afternoon.
Brown: Certainly, shall I tell him why? ....
Model: Yes, just tell him I've got an important board meeting, he'll understand.
Brown: Fine, I'll call him right away. ....
Model: Thank you.

White: Hallo, Peter White speaking. ....
Model: Hallo, Mr White. Have you got a moment?
White: Yes, Ms Green, of course. ....
Model: Well, I'd like you to phone Mr Grey and arrange an appointment for tomorrow lunchtime.
White: Certainly, shall I tell him what it's about? ....
Model: Yes, just tell him it's very important for both of us, he'll understand.
White: Right. I'll phone him right away. ....
Model: Thanks.

Scarlett: Hallo. Bob Scarlett speaking. ....
Model: Hallo, Mr Scarlett. Have you got a moment?
Scarlett: Yes, Ms Green, of course. ....
Model: Well, I'd like you to book a table for two at the Ritz for one o'clock tomorrow.
Scarlett: Certainly, shall I ask them for any particular table? ....
Model: Yes, just tell them I'd like my usual table, they'll understand.
Scarlett: Certainly, I'll get on to them now. ....
Model: Thanks.

Pink: Hallo. This is Mr Pink speaking ....
Model: Hallo, Mr Pink, can you do something for me, pleas
Pink: Yes, Ms Green. ....
Model: Well, I'd like you to ring the florist's and ask them t send Mr Grey a dozen roses.
Pink: Certainly, is there any message they should put on the card? ....
Model: Yes, just tell them to send my usual card, they'll understand.
Pink: Alright, I'll ring them right away. ....
Model: Thanks.

Silver: Hallo. Simon Silver. ....
Model: Hallo, Mr Silver, have you got a moment?
Silver: Yes, Ms Green? ....
Model: Well, I'd like you to tell the rest of the staff I mustn' be disturbed tomorrow afternoon.
Silver: Certainly, shall I tell them why? ....
Model: Yes, just tell them I've got an important meeting wit Mr Grey, they'll understand.
Silver: Alright, but I'm not sure they *will* understand. ....
Model: Just tell them! Alright?
Silver: Alright.

And that's the end of exercise 3.

Exercise 4 Asking your friends to do you a favour

Cassette 1 Side 2

This time you're going to hear friends talking. Look at your workbook and listen.

Michael: I'm just off to the shops.
Model: Are you going past the tobacconist's by any chance, Michael?
Michael: Yes, I think so.
Model: Well, do you think you could get me a kitchen-size box of matches?
Michael: What do you want such a large box for?
Model: Well, I always lose small boxes, you see.
Michael: OK. I'll do that.
Model: Thanks.

Jan: I'm just going shopping. Do you want anything?
Model: Are you going past the baker's by any chance, Jan?
Jan: Yes.

Model: Well, I wonder if you could get me fifteen Danish pastries.
Jan: Fifteen? What on earth do you want so many for?
Model: Well, I want to give everyone in the class one for tea.
Jan: OK. I hope I'll get one of them!
Model: Of course, thanks a lot.

Now you ask each of your friends in the same way. Ready? Start by asking Michael to get you some matches.

Michael: I'm just off to the shops. Want anything? ....
Model: Are you going past the tobacconist's by any chance, Michael?
Michael: Yes, I suppose so. ....
Model: Well, do you think you could get me a kitchen-size box of matches?
Michael: What do you want such a large box for? ....
Model: Well, I always lose small boxes, you see.
Michael: OK, then. ....
Model: Thanks.

Jan: Do you want anything from the shops? ....
Model: Are you going past the baker's by any chance, Jan?
Jan: Yes. ....
Model: Well, I wonder if you could get me fifteen Danish pastries.
Jan: Fifteen? I can't imagine why you want fifteen! ....
Model: Well, I want to give everyone in the class one for tea.
Jan: OK! You'll give me one, won't you? ....
Model: Of course, thanks a lot.

Rob: I'm just going down to the library. ....
Model: Are you going past the bank by any chance, Rob?
Rob: I might be. Why? ....
Model: Well, do you think you could pay this cheque into my account for me?
Rob: Why can't you do it yourself? ....
Model: Well, you see I've got a lot of phone calls to make.
Rob: Oh alright. Let's have it. ....
Model: Here you are. Thanks.

Anne: I'm just going out to lunch. ....
Model: Are you going past the chemist's by any chance, Anne?
Anne: Probably, yes, why? ....
Model: Well, could you possibly get me some aspirins?

Anne: What do you want aspirins for? ....
Model: Well, I've got a splitting headache, you see.
Anne: OK, sure. ....
Model: Thanks a lot.

Dave: I've got to go to the supermarket. ....
Model: Are you going past the bookshop by any chance, Dave?
Dave: I could do, but why? ....
Model: Well, do you think you could get a copy of that book you mentioned the other day?
Dave: What on earth for? ....
Model: Well, it's for you – it's your birthday present.
Dave: Oh, that's very nice, will you give me the money to get it? ....
Model: Of course, here you are.
Dave: Thanks ever so much. ....
Model: That's alright. Happy Birthday!

Happy end of exercise 4.

Exercise 5 Refusing to do something politely

The model answers are for guidance only – in the exercise you should make your own excuses. Listen to these examples first:

Acquaintance 1: Go and get me some cigarettes!
Model: I can't really, I'm in the middle of a lesson.

Acquaintance 2: Could you lend me £10?
Model: I'm very sorry, but I haven't got any money on me. Try someone else.

Now, let's start again. Give your own reasons for refusing each time. Imagine you're talking to acquaintances.

Acquaintance 1: Can you go and get me some cigarettes? ....
Model: Not really, I'm in the middle of a lesson, you see.
Acquaintance 1: Oh, OK.

Acquaintance 2: I say, you can't lend me £10, can you? ....
Model: No, I'm afraid not, I haven't got any money on me. You'd better try someone else.
Acquaintance 2: Alright.

Acquaintance 1:	I say, you're going to London by car, aren't you? Can you give me a lift? ....
Model:	I'm afraid I can't, the car's full already, you see.
Acquaintance 1:	Oh dear, thanks anyway.
Acquaintance 2:	Oh, by the way, can you lend me your dictionary for the evening? ....
Model:	No, I'm sorry, I'd rather not. I need it myself, you see.
Acquaintance 2:	Oh, I see. Never mind.
Acquaintance 1:	Could you possibly give me a light, do you think? ....
Model:	Well no, not really. You see, smoking isn't allowed in here.
Acquaintance 1:	Oh! I didn't feel like a cigarette really, anyway.
Acquaintance 2:	Hey! Open the window please! ....
Model:	Well, I don't think it's a good idea. It's very draughty already.
Acquaintance 2:	Really? Oh.
Acquaintance 1:	Excuse me. Sorry to trouble you and all that, but I wonder if you could possibly lend me your pen for a moment. ....
Model:	I'm ever so sorry, I'd like to, but it doesn't work properly.
Acquaintance 1:	Oh, never mind.
Acquaintance 2:	Have you got the correct time? ....
Model:	I'm afraid not, my watch has stopped. I'm sorry.
Acquaintance 2:	Oh, it doesn't really matter.
Acquaintance 1:	Hallo! You know it's our teacher's birthday tomorrow. Well, we're collecting money to buy him a present from the class. ....
Model:	What a nice idea! Here's 50p – is that enough?
Acquaintance 1:	Oh yes, that's fine. Thanks very much.

That's the end of exercise 5.
For the communication activity you need a partner. Please look at your workbook for the instructions. If you're working in a language laboratory, call your teacher when you're ready for this.
That's the end of unit 3. Please rewind your tape now.

In the communication activity one student looks at activity X, while the other looks at activity G. Each student tries to get hi or her partner to help with face-lifting an old house or moving into a new flat. The activity practises getting people to do things, agreeing and refusing.

Unit 4 Talking about past events: remembering, describing experiences, imagining 'What if . . .'

In these exercises we're going to concentrate on talking about the past. As usual, the examples are printed in your workbook.

Exercise 1 Remembering

Listen to these examples:

Friend: Have you ever been to France?
Model: Yes, I remember quite clearly that I went there on holiday in 1965 and '66.
Friend: Whereabouts did you go?
Model: As far as I can remember, I visited Paris in '65 and Brittany in '66 – or was it the other way round? I can't remember exactly.

Friend: How about Spain? Ever been there?
Model: Yes, I remember quite clearly that I went there on business in 1967 and '68.
Friend: Whereabouts did you go?
Model: As far as I can remember, I visited Madrid in '67 and Barcelona in '68 – or was it the other way round? I can't remember exactly.

The countries you've been to are printed in your workbook. Follow the pattern and answer your friend's questions. Ready?

Friend: Have you ever been to France? ....
Model: Yes, I remember quite clearly that I went there on holiday in 1965 and '66.
Friend: Whereabouts did you go? ....
Model: As far as I can remember, I visited Paris in '65 and Brittany in '66 – or was it the other way round? I can't remember exactly.

Friend: How about Spain? Ever been there? ....
Model: Yes, I remember quite clearly that I went there on business in 1967 and '68.
Friend: Whereabouts did you go? ....
Model: As far as I can remember, I visited Madrid in '67 and Barcelona in '68 – or was it the other way round? I can't remember exactly.

Friend: And what about Switzerland? I expect you've been there. ....
Model: Yes, I remember quite clearly that I went there on holiday in 1969 and '70.
Friend: Whereabouts did you go? ....
Model: As far as I can remember, I visited Zurich in '69 and Geneva in '70 – or was it the other way round? I can't remember exactly.

Friend: OK. Have you ever been to Canada? ....
Model: Yes, I remember quite clearly that I went there to visit my relations in 1971 and '72.
Friend: Whereabouts did you go? ....
Model: As far as I can remember, I visited Montreal in '71 and Toronto in '72 – or was it the other way round? I can't remember exactly.

Friend: Now then . . . Italy. Have you spent any time in Italy? ....
Model: Yes, I remember quite clearly that I went there for short visits in 1973 and '74.
Friend: Whereabouts did you go? ....
Model: As far as I can remember, I visited Rome in '73 and Venice in '74 – or was it the other way round? I can't remember exactly.

Friend: I see, never mind. You've probably been to England quite often, haven't you? ....
Model: Yes, I remember quite clearly that I came to England to study English in 1975 and '76.
Friend: Whereabouts did you go? ....
Model: As far as I can remember, I went to London in '75 and Bournemouth in '76 – or was it the other way round? I can't remember exactly.
Friend: Did you have a good time? ....
Model: Oh,yes, I had a wonderful time!
Friend: Good!

End of exercise 1.

Exercise 2 Talking about previous activities and giving reasons

Listen to these examples:

Friend 1: Why didn't you have a meal with us last night?
Model: Well, you see, I'd already had a meal, so I wasn't really hungry.

Friend 2: Why didn't you come for a swim with us yesterday afternoon?
Model: Well, you see, I'd already been for a swim, so I was a bit tired.

Now please follow the pattern and give your reasons for not joining your friends. Ready?

Friend 1: Why didn't you have a meal with us last night? ....
Model: Well, you see, I'd already had a meal, so I wasn't really hungry.

Friend 2: Why didn't you come for a swim with us yesterday afternoon? ....
Model: Well, you see, I'd already been for a swim, so I was a bit tired.

Friend 1: Why didn't you come to see the film with us on Saturday? ....
Model: Well, you see, I'd already seen that film, so I didn't want to see it again.

Friend 2: Why didn't you come to hear the lecture with us on Friday? ....
Model: Well, you see, I'd already heard that lecture, so I didn't want to hear it again.

Friend 1: Why didn't you want to visit the art gallery with us on Sunday? ....
Model: Well, you see, I'd already visited the art gallery, so I didn't want to revisit it.

Friend 2: Why didn't you come to look round the cathedral with us at the weekend? ....
Model: Well, you see, I'd already looked round the cathedral, so I didn't want to look round it again.

Friend 1: Why didn't you read the book we all read? ....
Model: Well, you see, I'd already read that book, so I didn't want to reread it.

Friend 2: Why didn't you sit the exam we all took in June? ....
Model: Well, you see, I'd already passed it, so I didn't need to resit it.
Friend 2: Good for you! I hope *we* all pass.

End of exercise 2.

Exercise 3 Describing experiences

We'd like you to imagine you're someone who has tried many different things in your life – but you have succeeded in none of them. Listen to these examples:

Friend: Tell me. Have you ever been on the stage?
Model: That takes me back, yes. I'll never forget the time I appeared at the National Theatre.
Friend: Why, what happened?
Model: I couldn't remember my lines! It was very embarrassing!

Friend: And have you played much tennis?
Model: That takes me back, yes. I'll never forget the time I played at Wimbledon.
Friend: Why, what happened?
Model: I got knocked out in the first round! It was awfully embarrassing!

In your workbook you can see the newspaper headlines which described each of your exploits. Let's start the conversations from the beginning.

Friend: Tell me. Have you ever been on the stage? ....
Model: That takes me back, yes. I'll never forget the time I appeared at the National Theatre.
Friend: Why, what happened? ....
Model: I couldn't remember my lines! It was very embarrassing!

Friend: Have you played much tennis? ....
Model: That takes me back, yes. I'll never forget the time I played at Wimbledon.
Friend: Why, what happened? ....
Model: I got knocked out in the first round! It was awfully embarrassing!

Friend: Have you ever been on TV? ....
Model: That takes me back, yes. I'll never forget the time I had my own show on BBC 2.
Friend: Why, what happened? ....
Model: I lost my voice just before the show! It was very embarrassing!

Friend: Have you ever given a lecture? ....
Model: That takes me back, yes. I'll never forget the time I gave a lecture at Oxford University.
Friend: Why, what happened? ....
Model: Nobody came to hear me! It was awfully embarrassing!

Friend: Have you done any motor-racing? ....
Model: That takes me back, yes. I'll never forget the time I drove in the British Grand Prix at Brands Hatch.
Friend: Why, what happened? ....
Model: My car wouldn't start! It was terribly embarrassing!

Friend: Have you ever done any mountain-climbing? ....
Model: That takes me back, yes. I'll never forget the time I climbed Mont Blanc.
Friend: Why, what happened? ....
Model: I had to be rescued by helicopter! It was extremely embarrassing.

Friend: And my last question. Have you done any sailing? ....
Model: That takes me back, yes. I'll never forget the time I sailed single-handed across the Atlantic.
Friend: Why, what happened? ....
Model: I was seasick all the time! It was a horrible experience!
Friend: You don't seem to have been very lucky in your life, do you? ....

End of exercise 3.

Exercise 4 On-going situations

In this exercise you'll be talking about arriving late for various events which your friends were on time for. Please listen carefully to these examples:

Friend: Did you arrive at school on time for the first lesson?
Model: I'm afraid not. By the time I arrived, the others were having their second lesson.
Friend: Really?

Model: Yes, I was so late that the first lesson had finished and the second had already started.

Friend: Did you get to the theatre on time for the first act?
Model: I'm afraid I didn't. By the time I got there, the others were watching the second act.
Friend: Really?
Model: Yes, I was so late that the first act had finished and the second had already started.

Now, follow the pattern and answer the questions yourself. Ready?

Friend: Did you arrive at school on time? ....
Model: I'm afraid not. By the time I arrived, the others were having their second lesson.
Friend: Really? ....
Model: Yes, I was so late that the first lesson had finished and the second had already started.

Friend: Did you get to the theatre on time? ....
Model: I'm afraid I didn't. By the time I got there, the others were watching the second act.
Friend: Really? ....
Model: Yes, I was so late that the first act had finished and the second had already started.

Friend: Did you manage to get to the park on time to play in the first half of the hockey match? ....
Model: I'm afraid not. By the time I arrived, the others were already playing the second half.
Friend: Really? ....
Model: Yes, I was so late that the first half had finished and the second had already started.

Friend: But you got to the law court in time to see the first case? ....
Model: No, I didn't I'm afraid. By the time I managed to get there, the others were watching the second case.
Friend: Really? ....
Model: Yes, I was so late that the first case had finished and the second had already started.

Friend: But of course you heard all the lectures in that conference you attended? ....
Model: I'm afraid not, by the time I arrived, the others were listening to the second lecture.

Friend: Really? ....
Model: Yes, I was so late that the first lecture had finished and the second had already started.
Friend: Well, you must try to be more punctual, mustn't you?
....
Model: Yes, I suppose so.

End of exercise 4.

Exercise 5 Imagining 'What if . . .'

Imagine you went on a motoring holiday and had a marvellous time. Nothing went wrong. Everything went right. Listen to the examples:

Friend: What would you have done if your car had broken down?
Model: Difficult to say, but I think I'd have taken it to a garage and asked them to fix it.

Friend: What would you have done if it'd rained all the time?
Model: Oh, I don't know, I suppose I might have come home early.

Now answer the questions yourself. The model answers are for guidance only, so don't worry if your answers are totally different. Ready?

Friend: What would you have done if your car had broken down? ....
Model: Difficult to say, but I think I'd have taken it to a garage and asked them to fix it.

Friend: What would you have done if it'd rained all the time?
....
Model: Oh, I don't know, I suppose I might have come home early.

Friend: What would you have done if you'd got lost? ....
Model: Difficult to say, but I think I'd have stopped to ask someone the way.

Friend: What would you have done if you'd run out of petrol?
....
Model: Difficult to say, but I suppose I'd have had to walk to the nearest petrol station.

Friend: What would you have done if you'd spent all your money? ....

Model: Oh, I don't know, I suppose I might have tried to phone my bank.

Friend: What would you have done if you'd been unable to find accommodation? ....

Model: Difficult to say, but I suppose I'd have slept in the car.

Friend: And how would you have felt the next day if you'd slept in your car? ....

Model: Difficult to say, but I suppose I'd have felt pretty cold and miserable.

Friend: What would you have done if your passport had been stolen? ....

Model: I don't know, but I suppose I might have gone to the police station and asked them for advice.

Friend: What would you have done if you hadn't been able to make people understand you? ....

Model: Difficult to say, but I suppose I'd have had to use sign language.

Friend: How would you have felt if your car had been stolen while you were on the beach? ....

Model: That's hard to say, but I think I'd have felt pretty helpless.

Friend: It's a good job it didn't happen then, isn't it? ....

Model: It certainly is!

End of exercise 5.
There is a communication activity for which you need to find a partner. The instructions are printed in your workbook. Call your teacher if you're working in a language laboratory.
End of unit 4.

In the communication activity, one student looks at activity U, while the other looks at activity N. One student has been to Scotland on holiday, the other to Devon and Cornwall. Each has to describe the trip to the other and the route has to be drawn on a map. This activity practises talking about past activities and experiences.

Unit 5 Conversation techniques: hesitating, preventing interruptions and interrupting politely, bringing in other people

Exercise 1 Hesitating while you think what to say

Listen to these examples:

Acquaintance 1: What do you think of this town?
Model: Er, well, how shall I put it? Um, it's alright really I suppose – perhaps you could say it's, you know, sort of provincial.

Acquaintance 2: What's the best restaurant in town?
Model: Well, actually, er, I'm not sure exactly what you mean by the 'best'. My favourite restaurant is called . . .

Now imagine some acquaintances are firing questions at you. Answer them as well as you can – use hesitation devices if you are not sure what to say. There aren't any model answers in this exercise. Ready?

Acquaintance 1: What do you think of this town? ....
Acquaintance 2: What's the best restaurant in town? ....
Acquaintance 1: What are the full names of your two best friends? ....
Acquaintance 2: What did you have for dinner the day before yesterday? ....
Acquaintance 1: What are you planning to do tomorrow evening? ....
Acquaintance 2: Describe the house you're living in at the moment. ....
Acquaintance 1: What do you enjoy most about studying English? ....
Acquaintance 2: How do you feel about using these exercises? ....
Acquaintance 1: That's all. Thanks very much. Er, by the way, do you want to ask *me* anything? ....

End of exercise 1

Exercise 2 Pretending to hesitate to show tentativeness or politeness

Listen to these two conversations:

Acquaintance: Do these sunglasses suit me?
Inappropriate answer: No, they don't.

Acquaintance: Do these sunglasses suit me?
Model: Well, actually, um, not really, no.

Which answer seemed more pleasant? ....
Yes, a fast answer to a question sometimes sounds abrupt or superior or arrogant. It's often better to be less direct by pretending to hesitate. Listen to another example:

Acquaintance: Is this the right road for Salisbury?
Model: Er, no, actually you've taken the wrong turning.

Now answer *No* to these questions. The model answers are for guidance only. Try to sound pleasant by pretending to hesitate:

Acquaintance: Do these sunglasses suit me? ....
Model: Well, actually, they, um, don't really flatter you.

Acquaintance: Is this the right road for London? ....
Model: Um, well, in fact, the thing is I think you must have taken a wrong turning.

Acquaintance: Can you read my handwriting? ....
Model: Er, it's sort of a bit difficult to read *every* word.

Acquaintance: Am I speaking clearly enough? ....
Model: Well, how shall I put it? I can't, er, understand you all that well.

Acquaintance: Did you enjoy the meal I cooked for you? ....
Model: Well, the thing is, I'm not too keen on, er, vegetarian food. Sorry.

Acquaintance: Is this seat free? ....
Model: Er, well, actually, I'm waiting for a friend.

Acquaintance: Haven't you finished your coffee yet? ....
Model: Er, no, it's you know, a bit, er, hot so I'm sort of waiting.

Acquaintance: Are you coming out with me tonight? ....
Model: Er, well, no, actually, I can't. I've arranged to go out with Peter.

Acquaintance: Don't you *ever* say yes? ....
Model: Er, well, actually I, um, don't very often, you see.

End of exercise 2.

Exercise 3 Breaking into a conversation

Look at your workbook and listen to these examples:

Anne: Got any plans for the weekend, Bill? Are you going anywhere?

Bill: Well, I wanted to go to London, but I can't afford the train fare.

Model: By the way, I'm driving to London on Sunday. Would you like a lift?

Bill: That's nice, yes, thanks very much. The problem is that I've sort of arranged to see Peter on Sunday now and I don't want to let him down.

Anne: No, he was saying to me how much he was looking forward to . . . Sorry, did you want to say something?

Model: Yes, sorry to interrupt, but which Peter do you mean? Are you talking about Peter Hill or Peter Brown?

Now let's start the conversation again. Imagine you are talking to some friends. Interrupt at the appropriate moments to make the points listed in your workbook.

Anne: Got any plans for the weekend?

Bill: Well, I had planned to go to London, but I can't afford the train fare. ....

Model: By the way, I'm driving to London on Sunday. Would you like a lift?

Bill: That's very kind of you, but I've just arranged to spend the day with Peter.

Anne: I know Peter, he's a very . . . Sorry . . . .

Model: Sorry to interrupt, but which Peter do you mean? Are you talking about Peter Hill or Peter Brown?

Anne: Peter Brown – I don't think I know the other one. Anyway, as I was saying, he's a very . . . Sorry, you wanted to ask Bill something. ....

Model: Yes, by the way, Bill, I was wondering if you *and* Peter would like to come to London?

Bill: Oh, that's very kind of you, but I happen to know that Peter hates being driven anywhere – nothing personal of course. He had a nasty accident on the way to Scotland once, you see. ....

Model: By the way, I went to Scotland last summer – it was really nice there.

Anne: I'm surprised to hear that – everyone else I've talked to said it was awful there – you know, the weather, the food, the . . . .

Model: Sorry to interrupt, but I don't really agree. When I was there the weather was lovely and the food delicious.
Bill: I've never been there, of course, but I've read about the heavy industry and pollution in parts of Scotland. And the influence of all this North Sea oil must be dreadful.
....
Model: Oh, by the way, that reminds me, I saw a very interesting film on TV about North Sea oil.
Anne: Oh, did you?
Bill: Yes, I expect it told you a lot about all the pollution that's been caused and the way in which . . . .
Model: Sorry to interrupt again, but that's just not true: the oil companies have made great efforts to protect the environment in Scotland.
Bill: Oh, I see, sorry. Anyway, to change the subject, Anne, any ideas for this evening? Can you think of a nice restaurant?
Anne: Um, no . . . .
Model: By the way, I went to an excellent Chinese place the other day.
Anne: Oh, no. I can't stand Chinese food. You get a big plate of something and it's really boring – there's no variety . . . .
Model: Sorry to interrupt, but I'd just like to say that if everyone in the group orders different things you can share all the different dishes.
Anne: Oh, yes! I've never thought of that.
Bill: Mmm! Good idea. By the way, would you like to join us this evening? ....
Model: No, I'd rather not if you don't mind. I've got quite a lot of work to do. Perhaps some other time.
Anne: OK. I must be off, you two. Bye!
Bill: Me too. Bye! ....
Model: Bye, see you soon.

That's the end of exercise 3.

Exercise 4 Being brought into a conversation

In this exercise the other speakers will bring you into the conversation by asking for your comments or opinions. Like this, listen:

Anne: Well, I must say life in Britain is quite different from what I'm used to. Take the traffic for example. British drivers seem to drive much more aggressively than drivers in my country.

Bill: Yes, I quite agree. But what do you think, Pat? What's your experience? ....

Bill: Hmm, I see. Another thing that's different is the food. English food is very . . . how shall I say . . . how would you describe English food, Pat? ....

Now let's start the conversation again. Make your own comments when the speakers bring you into the conversation. Your name is Pat. There are no model answers.

Anne: Well, life in Britain seems very strange to me. Take British drivers, for example. ....

Bill: Yes, I know what you mean. They're so aggressive, aren't they? Pat, what's your experience? ....

Bill: Hmm, I see. Another thing that's quite strange is the food. Pat, how would you describe English food? ....

Bill: Yes, I see what you mean.

Anne: Oh yes, that reminds me of the meal I had on my birthday. Normally I hate birthdays.

Bill: Yes, so do I.

Anne: This meal was fantastic. There were five courses and we all had champagne and got very drunk.

Bill: I think that's shocking, don't you, Pat? ....

Anne: That's just nonsense, I'm afraid. You don't know what you're talking about, Pat! ....

Bill: OK. Let's change the subject. Um, another thing I can't get used to is this English weather. Rain one day, sunshine the next.

Anne: I know. It's extraordinary, isn't it?

Bill: Mmm. Yes. No wonder the typical Englishman always carries an umbrella.

Anne: Ha ha, yes.

Bill: You're very quiet, Pat. ....

Anne: Sorry to interrupt, but before I forget, have either of you ever spent an evening with an English family that doesn't watch TV at some stage in the evening?

Bill: No I haven't. They all seem obsessed with TV, don't you agree, Pat? ....

Bill: I don't know what *you* think, Pat, but in my experience some TV programmes are really very good indeed ....

Anne: That's a funny thing to say. What do you mean exactly, Pat? ....

Anne: I still don't see what you mean, I'm afraid. Perhaps I'm being stupid. ....
Anne: I see! Yes! Well I must be off, I've got some homework to do. I seem to spend hours on my homework every evening.
Bill: Yes, so do I hours and hours!
Anne: Just a minute, Pat's looking sceptical. Don't you believe us, Pat? ....
Anne: Well, I've really got to go. Bye.
Bill: Bye! Bye, Pat! ....

End of exercise 4.

Exercise 5 Without making notes or preparing yourself, give a one-minute talk about your country. Use a blank tape for your recording. That's the end of unit 5.

There is no communication activity for this unit, but exercise 5 practises speaking freely for one minute.

Unit 6 Talking about the future: stating intentions, discussing probability, considering 'What if. . .'

Exercise 1 Stating intentions

Cassette 2 Side 1

Please look at your workbook, which shows your plans for the next few days. ....
Now, listen to these examples:

Friend 1: Are you going to phone home?
Model: I haven't made up my mind whether to phone home.

Friend 2: Are you planning to play tennis one afternoon this week?
Model: Yes, I'm certainly going to play tennis.

OK? Let's begin. Don't worry if your answer is different from the model answer – there are of course *several* ways of stating your intentions.

Friend 1: Are you going to phone home? ....
Model: I haven't made up my mind whether to phone home.

Friend 2: Are you planning to play tennis at all? ....
Model: Yes, I'm certainly going to play tennis.

Friend 1: Are you going to go to London tomorrow? ....
Model: No, I'm certainly *not* going to go to London tomorrow.

Friend 2: Are you going to write a letter home this week? ....
Model: No, I don't really feel like writing a letter home.

Friend 1: Are you going to prepare for tomorrow's lesson? ....
Model: Yes, I may well prepare for tomorrow's lesson.

Friend 2: There's a good film at the ABC – are you going? ....
Model: No, I shouldn't think I'll go to it.

Friend 1: Are you going to watch TV tomorrow night? ....
Model: Yes, I thought I might watch TV.

Friend 2: Are you coming for a drink after this lesson? ....
Model: Yes, I should think I'll come – it depends on how I feel.

Friend 1: Are you going to go for a run tomorrow morning? ....
Model: No, you won't catch me going for a run – not in the morning, anyway!

Friend 2: Are you going to come to English lessons next week? ....
Model: Oh yes, nothing's going to stop me coming to English lessons.
Friend 2: I'm glad to hear it!

End of exercise 1.

Exercise 2 Discussing probability

Please look at your workbook, which shows the probability or improbability of various events happening next year. ....
Now, please listen to the examples:

Friend 1: Do you think the weather next summer will be better than this summer?
Model: Yes, it's bound to be better next summer.

Friend 2: Is there any chance of the government changing next year?
Model: No, I'm absolutely sure there won't be a new government next year.

If you're ready, we'll begin.

Friend 1: This summer's weather is awful. Do you think it'll be better next summer? ....
Model: Yes, it's bound to be better next summer.

Friend 2: I read that we might have a change of government next year. What do you think? ....
Model: I'm absolutely sure we won't have a new government next year.

Friend 1: I've heard income tax is going to be reduced next year. Do you think it will be? ....
Model: Yes, there's a chance it'll be reduced.

Friend 2: And VAT's supposed to be going up again. Is that likely, do you think? ....
Model: Yes, I suppose VAT might go up again.

Friend 1: I heard a rumour that the Queen's going to abdicate next year. Is it true? ....
Model: No, of course she won't abdicate!

Friend 2: I did hear that train fares might go down – to encourage people to travel by rail. Is that likely? ....
Model: No, I doubt if train fares will go down.

Friend 1: Everyone says prices will go on rising. What do you say? ....
Model: Yes, I expect prices will go on rising – as usual.

Friend 2: I think England are sure to win the next World Cup, don't you? ....
Model: No, there's not much chance of England winning the World Cup.

Friend 1: They say that the crime rate is rising this year. How about next year? ....
Model: I wouldn't be surprised if it rose again next year.

Friend 2: Your English is very good now. Will it be even better next year? ....
Model: Yes, my English is sure to be better next year!
Friend 2: Yes, I'm sure it will – mind you, you've got to keep practising of course!

End of exercise 2.

Exercise 3 The consequences of possible or probable future events

In this exercise we're going to talk about events which might possibly happen or which are probably going to happen. Listen to these examples:

Friend: Now, you're going to take the exam in June, aren't you? How will you feel if you pass?
Model: Well, I suppose I'll feel very pleased.

Friend: And what will you do when you hear you've passed?
Model: I think I'll throw a party – I'll invite all my friends to celebrate.

Right! Let's start again from the beginning. Use your own ideas to answer the questions and we'll give you a model answer just for comparison. Ready?

Friend: Right. This exam in June. You've worked hard, you have a good chance of passing. How will you feel if you do pass? ....
Model: Well, I suppose I'll feel very pleased.

Friend: Uhhu. And what will you do if you pass? ....
Model: I'll throw a party – I'll invite all my friends to celebrate.

Friend: OK. But you might be unlucky. You might fail the exam. How will you feel if you fail? ....
Model: Well, I suppose I'll be very disappointed.

Friend: And what will you do if you fail? Give up learning English? ....
Model: No, I'll take the exam again next year.

Friend: How will you feel if the weather's bad this weekend? ....
Model: Well, I suppose I'll feel a bit depressed.

Friend: What will you do if the weather's bad? ....
Model: I'll stay at home and do some reading.

Friend: On the other hand, it might be fine this weekend. How will you feel if the weather's fine? ....
Model: Well, I suppose I'll be in a good mood.

Friend: And what will you do? ....
Model: I'll go out and take advantage of the good weather.

Friend: Now, you're going out this evening, aren't you? How will you feel if you miss the last bus home? ....
Model: Well, I suppose I'll feel pretty angry with myself.

Friend: And what will you do? ....
Model: I'll have to get a taxi, I suppose.

Friend: I guess that'll be quite expensive, won't it? ....
Model: Yes, it certainly will!

End of exercise 3.

Exercise 4 Speculating about unlikely or impossible events

This time we're going to talk about events that are extremely unlikely to happen, or which are clearly impossible. Listen:

Friend: How would you feel if you were thrown into prison tomorrow?
Model: Oh, I expect I'd feel pretty indignant.

Friend: And what would you do if that happened?
Model: Oh, I suppose I'd get a good lawyer to defend me in court.

Now, it's your turn to speculate how *you* would feel and what *you* would do. Use your own ideas. The model answers are for guidance only. Ready?

Friend: How would you feel if you were arrested by the police? ....
Model: Oh, I expect I'd feel pretty indignant.

Friend: And what would you do? ....
Model: Oh, I suppose I'd get a good lawyer to defend me in court.

Friend: How would you feel if a world war broke out suddenly? ....
Model: Oh, I suppose I'd feel absolutely terrified.

Friend: And what would you do? ....
Model: Oh, I suppose I'd just stay at home, listening to the radio, hoping we weren't bombed.

Friend: On a lighter note. How would you feel if your family paid you a surprise visit at the weekend? ....
Model: Oh, I expect I'd be really pleased.

Friend: And what would you do? ....
Model: Oh, I suppose I'd take them out to show them the town – we'd certainly have a good meal, anyway.

Friend: How would you feel if today was a public holiday? ....
Model: Oh, I expect I'd feel at a bit of a loose end. I wouldn't have made any plans.

Friend: What would you do, then? ....
Model: Oh, I suppose I'd find something to do, maybe go out for a walk.

Friend: How would you feel if your car was a total write-off? If you'd left it parked in the street and the next morning it was wrecked? ....
Model: Oh, I expect I'd feel absolutely furious.

Friend: And what would you do, do you think? ....
Model: Oh, I suppose I'd report it to the police and see if they could find out who was responsible. Otherwise I'd just have to claim on my insurance.

Friend: But what if you weren't insured? What would you do? ....
Model: Hmm, that's a very good question. I really don't know what I'd do.

Friend: One last question: what would you do if you had lost your memory? If you couldn't even remember your own name? ....
Model: Oh, I suppose I'd try to find someone who knew me, who could tell me all about myself. Or I *could* try a doctor, perhaps.
Friend: I see. OK.

That's the end of exercise 4.

Exercise 5 Reacting to the unexpected

In this exercise you're going to be asked various questions about the future. There are no model answers – use your own ideas to answer the questions. Here's an example:

Friend: Do you think it's going to rain today?
Model: Mmm, I wouldn't be surprised if it rained.

OK? Now answer the questions yourself.

Friend: Do you think the weather's going to improve this week? ....
Friend: What are you going to do when your English course has finished? ....
Friend: Have you got any plans for the weekend? ....
Friend: How would you feel if you won first prize on a TV quiz show? ....
Friend: What are you having for lunch tomorrow? ....
Friend: What would you do if you lost your job? ....
Friend: Is there any chance of your getting a pay rise next year? ....
Friend: How are you planning to celebrate your birthday? ....
Friend: And what presents are you hoping to get on your birthday? ....
Friend: One last question: what are you going to do when you finish working on this unit? ....

That's the end of exercise 5.
There's a communication activity for you to do with a partner when you've finished work on the exercises. The instructions are printed in your workbook. Call your teacher if you're working in a language laboratory.
End of unit 6.

In the communication activity, one student looks at activity A, while the other looks at activity J. Both students are planning to spend one week in London together, but each has different plans. The activity practises talking about intentions.

Unit 7 Offering to do something, asking permission, giving reasons

Exercise 1 Offering to help a friend

Listen to these examples:

Friend 1: I'm ever so hungry.
Model: If you like, I could go and get you something to eat. How about a sandwich?
Friend 1: Mmm. Thanks a lot.

Friend 2: I'm awfully thirsty.
Model: Let me get you something to drink. How about some lemonade?
Friend 2: Oh yes, thanks ever so much.

Imagine you're talking to friends. Offer to help them when the mention each of their little problems. Use your own ideas each time. The model answers are for guidance only. Try to use different ways of offering each time. Ready?

Friend 1: I'm terribly hungry. ....
Model: If you like, I could go and get you someting to eat. How about a sandwich?
Friend 1: Mmm. Thanks a lot.

Friend 2: I'm awfully thirsty. ....
Model: Let me get you something to drink. How about some lemonade?
Friend 2: Oh, that'd be lovely, thanks.

Friend 1: Ohh! I've got a splitting headache today. ....
Model: Shall I go and get you something for it. How about some aspirins?
Friend 1: Oh yes, please.

Friend 2: My nose is all stuffed up. ....
Model: If you like, I could go and get you something for it. How about some nasal spray?
Friend 2: Nasal spray? That's just what I need.

Friend 1: Brr! It's very cold today, isn't it? ....
Model: Any point in my going to get you something warm to wear? How about a pullover?
Friend 1: Oh yes, that's very kind of you.

Friend 2: Oh goodness, I haven't got any money on me! ....
Model: Let me lend you some money. Would a pound be enough?
Friend 2: I'd rather have a fiver. ....
Model: OK. Here you are.
Friend 2: Thanks.

Friend 1: I'm awfully fed up. ....
Model: If you like, I could try to cheer you up a bit. How about my telling you a joke?
Friend 1: No jokes thank you. It'd only make it worse. ....
Model: Alright. I just wanted to help.
Friend 1: Thanks, anyway.

End of exercise 1.

Exercise 2 Offering to help someone you don't know very well

Listen to these examples:

Acquaintance: My throat's a bit dry.
Model: Would you like me to go and get you something to drink? Perhaps a glass of water?
Acquaintance: That's very kind of you, thanks.

Acquaintance: I must say I do feel like a snack.
Model: Would you like me to go and get you something to eat? Perhaps a sandwich?
Acquaintance: That's very nice of you. Thanks very much.

Now it's your turn to make helpful offers. Imagine you're talking to someone you don't know very well. Again the model answers are for guidance only. Ready?

Acquaintance: My throat's rather dry, I'm afraid. ....
Model: Would you like me to go and get you something to drink? Perhaps a glass of water?
Acquaintance: That's very kind of you, thanks.

Acquaintance: I think I feel like a snack. I'm a bit hungry.
....
Model: Would you like me to go and get you something to eat? Perhaps a sandwich?
Acquaintance: That's very nice of you. Thanks very much.

Acquaintance: I've forgotten to bring anything to write with.
....
Model: Would you like me to go and get you something to write with? Perhaps a pencil?
Acquaintance: Would you really? Thanks ever so much.

Acquaintance: Oh bother, I've just torn this piece of paper by mistake. ....
Model: Would you like me to go and get you something to stick it back together with? Perhaps some sticky tape?
Acquaintance: Oh, yes please. Thanks very much.

Acquaintance: I can't break this piece of string. ....
Model: Would you like me to go and get you something to cut it with? Perhaps some scissors?
Acquaintance: Oh yes, that's very kind of you, thanks.

Acquaintance: I wish I had something to read. ....
Model: Would you like me to go and get you something to read? Perhaps a newspaper?
Acquaintance: Thanks very much indeed. I'd like the *Guardian* if they've got it.

Acquaintance: Your English is very good. I wish mine was as good as yours. ....
Model: Would you like me to recommend a good book? Perhaps *Functions of English*?
Acquaintance: *Functions of English*? Is it any good? ....
Model: Oh yes, it's a very useful book.
Acquaintance: Thanks very much for the recommendation.

End of exercise 2.

Exercise 3 Accepting offers

This time different people are going to offer to do things for you. Accept their offers appropriately. Your name is Kim Smith. Listen to these examples:

Friend: Hey, Kim, was that your tummy rumbling? Let me get you something to eat.
Model: Oh, thanks a lot. Can you get me a sandwich, please?

Acquaintance: Excuse me, Mr Smith, I'm just going to the canteen. Would you like me to get you something?
Model: Oh, that's very kind of you, thanks. I'd like a cheese sandwich, please.

Now please accept the following offers. The model answers are simply for guidance and for comparison afterwards.

Friend: Hey, Kim, you haven't eaten all day. Let me get you something to eat. ....
Model: Oh, thanks a lot. Can you get me a doughnut, please?

Acquaintance: Excuse me, Mr Smith, I'm just going to the canteen. Would you like me to get you something? ....
Model: Oh, that's very kind of you, thanks. I'd like a cheese sandwich, please.

Friend: I say, Kim, do you want anything from the shops? ....
Model: Oh, thanks a lot, yes I'd like a newspaper. Can you get me the *Guardian*, please?

Friend: Oh, Kim, do you want me to open the windows? ....
Model: Thanks a lot, yes please. Just a little, otherwise there'll be a draught.

Acquaintance: I'm making a pot of tea, Mr Smith. Would you like me to bring you a cup when it's ready? ....
Model: That's very kind of you thanks. I'd like it with milk and no sugar, please.

Acquaintance: Um, Mr Smith, I'm going to the post office. Would you like me to post anything for you? ....
Model: That's very kind of you, thanks. Could you possibly get a stamp for this letter, please?

Friend: Let me get you a drink, Kim. ....
Model: Thanks a lot. Can you get me a half of lager, please?

End of exercise 3.

Exercise 4 Refusing offers

In this exercise we'd like you to *refuse* the offers appropriately. Like this, listen:

Friend: Let me get you a drink, Kim.
Model: No, it's alright, I haven't finished this one yet. Thanks all the same.

Acquaintance: Would you like me to get you a drink, Mr Smith?
Model: Oh that's very kind of you, but I haven't quite finished this one.

Alright? Let's start:

Friend: Shall I get you a drink, Kim? ....
Model: No, it's alright. I haven't finished this one yet. Thanks all the same.

Acquaintance: Would you like me to get you a drink, Mr Smith? ....
Model: Oh, that's very kind of you, but I haven't quit finished this one.

Acquaintance: That suitcase looks very heavy, Mr Smith. Would you like me to carry it for you? ....
Model: No, it's quite alright I can manage. Thank you for offering, though.

Friend: Oh, Kim, I'm going to the launderette. Do you want me to do your washing for you? ....
Model: No, don't bother, I can do it myself this evening. Thanks all the same.

Acquaintance: I'm sorry to hear you've left your books at home, Mr Smith, would you like me to go and get them? ....
Model: Thanks ever so much, but it's alright really. I think I can manage without them.

Friend: Is that all the money you've got, Kim? Would you like me to lend you some? ....
Model: No it's alright thanks. I think I've got enough at the moment. Thanks all the same.

Friend: Oh come on, Kim, I insist. You've only got 50p and I've got plenty of money. Here, let me give you £10. ....
Model: No, really, it's alright. I can manage till tomorrow. Thanks, though.

Friend: Now I'm not going to take No for an answer. Here's £10. Pay me back when you can! ....
Model: Oh alright. Thanks a lot.

End of exercise 4.

Exercise 5 Asking friends for permission and giving reasons

In this exercise we'd like you to ask some friends for permission to do various things. Look at your workbook, and listen to these examples:

Susan: If you want to open the window, you'd better ask John.
Model: I say, John, d'you mind if I open the window?
John: What for?

Model: Well, you see, it's a bit stuffy in here and I've got a bit of a headache.
John: Oh, yes, sure, go ahead.

Susan: If you want to smoke a cigarette, you'd better ask Mary.
Model: I say, Mary, is it alright if I have a cigarette?
Mary: Why?
Model: Well, you see, I'm feeling a bit tense and a cigarette will calm me down.
Mary: Yes, go ahead, I don't mind.

Now ask permission yourself and invent a good reason each time – we'll suggest one in the model answer for comparison afterwards. Imagine you and your friends are together in your flat.

Susan: If you want to open the window, you'd better ask John. ....
Model: I say, John, d'you mind if I open the window?
John: What for? ....
Model: Well, you see, it's a bit stuffy in here and I've got a bit of a headache.
John: Yes, sure, go ahead.

Susan: If you want to smoke a cigarette, you'd better ask Mary. ....
Model: I say, Mary, is it alright if I have a cigarette?
Mary: Why? ....
Model: Well, you see, I'm feeling a bit tense and it'll calm me down.
Mary: Yes, that's alright. I don't mind.

Susan: If you want to turn on the television, you'd better ask John. ....
Model: I say, John, is it alright if I turn on the television?
John: What's on? ....
Model: Well, you see, there's a good film on BBC 1 I'd like to watch.
John: OK, go ahead.

Susan: If you'd like to turn off the radio I think you should ask Mary. ....
Model: I say, Mary, do you mind if I turn off the radio?
Mary: Why? ....
Model: Well, you see, I'd like to watch something on TV.
Mary: OK.

John: If you want to draw the curtains, you'd better ask Susan. ....

Model: I say, Susan, I'm going to draw the curtains. Is that alright with you?

Susan: But I'm trying to read. ....

Model: Well, you see, I want to see this film on TV and the sun's shining on the screen.

Susan: Oh alright. But I'd like the light on and if you want to put on the light, you'd better make sure everyone else agrees. ....

Model: I say, everyone, does anyone mind if I put on the light?

All: What for? ....

Model: Well, you see, Susan wants to read and I've just drawn the curtains.

All: Yes, go ahead.

End of exercise 5.

Exercise 6 Asking your boss for permission and giving reasons

This time you'll be asking your boss for permission to do variou things. Listen to these examples:

Colleague: You'd better ask Mr Brown if you want to bring your dog to the office tomorrow.

Model: Excuse me, Mr Brown, I hope you don't mind, but would it be possible for me to bring my dog to the office tomorrow?

Mr Brown: Your dog? What for?

Model: Well, you see, he gets very lonely at home and I fee so sorry for him.

Mr Brown: Well, I'm afraid you can't. Sorry.

Colleague: You'd better ask Mr Brown if you want to use his phone.

Model: Excuse me, Mr Brown, would it be alright if I used your phone?

Mr Brown: Why don't you use the public phone in the canteen?

Model: Well, you see, it's rather urgent and someone else is using the pay phone.

Mr Brown: Oh, alright.

Now ask Mr Brown for permission to do each thing. Imagine you're in the office. Ready?

Colleague: You'd better ask Mr Brown if you want to bring your dog to the office tomorrow. ....

Model: Excuse me, Mr Brown, I hope you don't mind, but would it be possible for me to bring my dog to the office tomorrow.

Mr Brown: Your dog? What for? ....

Model: Well, you see, he gets very lonely at home and I feel so sorry for him.

Mr Brown: Well, I'm afraid you can't. Sorry.

Colleague: You'd better ask Mr Brown if you want to use his phone. ....

Model: Excuse me, Mr Brown, would it be alright if I used your phone?

Mr Brown: Why don't you use the public phone in the canteen? ....

Model: Well, you see, it's out of order and I've got a rather urgent call to make.

Mr Brown: Oh alright.

Colleague: I think you ought to tell Mr Brown before you go out to lunch early. ....

Model: Excuse me, Mr Brown, would you mind if I went to lunch early?

Mr Brown: Why do you have to go early? ....

Model: Well, you see, I've arranged to meet my sister, we've got to buy my mother a birthday present.

Mr Brown: I see. Alright. But don't be late back.

Colleague: It'd be best to ask Mr Brown if you want to listen to the radio. ....

Model: Excuse me, Mr Brown, I wonder if I could possibly listen to the radio?

Mr Brown: The radio? Why? ....

Model: Well, you see, I'd like to hear the news – the result of the international match should be on.

Mr Brown: Huh! You and your football! Very well.

Colleague: See if Mr Brown minds before you go out to the tobacconist's. ....

Model: Excuse me, Mr Brown, is it alright if I go out to the tobacconist's?

Mr Brown: What for? ....

Model: Well, you see, I've run out of cigarettes.

Mr Brown: Oh well, alright. Get me a box of matches while you're there, please.

Colleague: You'd better ask Mr Brown if you want to go to the dentist's. ....
Model: Excuse me, Mr Brown is it alright if I go to the dentist's?
Mr Brown: What, now? No, it's the worst possible time. We'r very busy. Why now? ....
Model: Well, you see, I've got a terrible toothache and I really must have it seen to.
Mr Brown: Oh, I am sorry. Of course you can. Take the who day off if you don't feel any better.

End of exercise 6.
There's a communication activity, for which you need to find partner. Instructions are printed in your workbook. Call your teacher if you're working in a language laboratory.
End of unit 7.

In the communication activity, one student looks at activity W while the other looks at activity O. Both want to watch TV together this evening. First they mark independently what the want to see in the TV guide. Then they try to get each other's permission to watch this choice.

Unit 8 Giving opinions, agreeing and disagreeing, discussing

Exercise 1 Giving your opinion to a friend

In this exercise we're going to ask you for your opinion about the topics listed in your workbook. It might be a good idea to think about these before we begin. ....
Listen to these examples:

Friend: How do you feel about flying?
Model: Well, if you ask me, flying is one of the safest ways of travelling.
Friend: Why do you think that?
Model: Because if you compare flying with other ways of travelling, there are far fewer accidents.

Friend: What do you think about travelling by car?
Model: Well, as I see it, travelling by car is going to be less and less popular in the future.
Friend: What makes you say that?

Model: Because of the congestion on the roads and because petrol is going to be more and more expensive.

OK. Now, the model answers we'll give are for guidance only. Imagine a friend is asking for your views. Ready?

Friend: How do you feel about flying? ....
Model: Well, if you ask me, flying is one of the safest ways of travelling.
Friend: Why do you think that? ....
Model: Because if you compare flying with other means of transport, there are far fewer accidents.

Friend: What do you think about travelling by car? ....
Model: Well, as I see it, travelling by car is going to be less and less popular in the future.
Friend: What makes you say that? ....
Model: Because of the congestion on the roads and because petrol is going to be more and more expensive.

Friend: How do you feel about cycling? ....
Model: Well, if you ask me, cycling is one of the most pleasant ways of travelling.
Friend: Why do you think that? ....
Model: Because it's so healthy and it doesn't pollute the environment at all.

Friend: What are your views on going by coach? ....
Model: Well, the point is going by coach is an awful way to travel.
Friend: Really? What makes you say that? ....
Model: Because it's so claustrophobic – you can't stand up and walk around.

Friend: How about trains? ....
Model: Well, don't you agree that trains are one of the most efficient forms of transport?
Friend: In what way? ....
Model: Because they can carry very large numbers of people for fairly long distances at high speed.

Friend: And what about walking? ....
Model: Well, if you ask me, walking is the healthiest possible way of getting from A to B.
Friend: What makes you say that? ....
Model: Because you're dependent on your own energy and you can breathe fresh air.

Friend: But surely that only applies over very short distances?
....

Model: Mmm, I suppose you need other forms of transport for long-distance travel.

Friend: I quite agree.

End of exercise 1.

Exercise 2 Disagreeing politely with a stranger

A stranger is going to give you his views on Britain and the British. Disagree as politely as possible, like this:

Stranger: You know what I think, I think British weather is wonderful.
Model: I'm not sure I quite agree.
Stranger: Oh, what's your experience, then?
Model: All things considered, I'd say that it was a little unreliable.

Stranger: I believe that British people are very friendly to strangers.
Model: I'm not sure I quite agree.
Stranger: Oh, what's your experience, then?
Model: As I see it, I'd say that they were a little unfriendly.

Now disagree politely with the opinions you hear. Imagine you're talking to a stranger. Ready?

Stranger: You know what I think, I think British weather is wonderful. ....
Model: I'm not sure I quite agree.
Stranger: Oh, what's your experience, then? ....
Model: All things considered, I'd say that it was a bit unreliable.

Stranger: I believe that British people are very friendly to strangers. ....
Model: I'm not sure I quite agree.
Stranger: Oh, what's your experience, then? ....
Model: As I see it, I'd say they were a little difficult to get to know.

Stranger: It's a fact that British families hardly ever watch TV.
....

Model: I'm not sure I quite agree.

Stranger: Oh, what's your experience, then? ....
Model: All things considered, I'd say that they watch TV quite often.

Stranger: I can't help thinking that, compared with other cities, London is a very quiet city to live in. ....
Model: I'm not sure I quite agree.
Stranger: Oh, what's your experience, then? ....
Model: All things considered, I must say that it's quite a noisy city.

Stranger: The point is that English people and American people are very similar. ....
Model: I'm not sure I quite agree.
Stranger: Oh, what's your experience, then? ....
Model: I'd just like to say that I think they're very different.

Stranger: If you ask me, English is a very easy language to learn. ....
Model: I'm not sure I quite agree.
Stranger: Oh, what's your experience, then? ....
Model: All things considered, I'd say that it was quite difficult.
Stranger: I suppose it depends on how similar your own language is. ....
Model: Yes, exactly.

End of exercise 2.

Exercise 3 Agreeing with people

Cassette 2 Side 2

When we *agree* with people, we don't need to be so polite as when we disagree. Look at your workbook and listen to these examples:

Acquaintance: If you ask me, the best time for a holiday in Scotland is June.
Model: You know, that's exactly what I think.
Acquaintance: Really?
Model: Yes, the weather's generally good and there are fewer tourists there.

Acquaintance: As far as I'm concerned, there's no better month for a winter holiday in Austria than March.
Model: I couldn't agree more.
Acquaintance: Really?
Model: Yes, the days are getting longer and the skiing is generally better.

Now it's your turn to agree with what you hear and give reaso for your opinion. Try to find a different way to agree each tim Ready?

Acquaintance: It seems to me that the best time for a holida in Scotland is June. ....
Model: You know, that's exactly what I think.
Acquaintance: Really? ....
Model: Yes, the weather's generally good and there ar fewer tourists there.

Acquaintance: As far as I'm concerned, there's no better tim for a winter holiday in Austria than March. ....
Model: I couldn't agree more.
Acquaintance: Really? ....
Model: Yes, the days are getting longer and the skiing is generally better.

Acquaintance: Wouldn't you say that the best month for a holiday in Greece is May? ....
Model: Yes, I entirely agree.
Acquaintance: Really? ....
Model: Yes, the weather's generally not too hot and there are fewer visitors around.

Acquaintance: It seems to me that if you're going to Spain, you've really got to go in September. ....
Model: You know, that's exactly what I think.
Acquaintance: Really? ....
Model: Yes, the weather's generally warm and the beaches are much less crowded.

Acquaintance: I'd say that there's no better time to visit the Alps than July. ....
Model: I couldn't agree more.
Acquaintance: Really? ....
Model: Yes, the weather's generally warm and dry and the mountains are at their best.

Acquaintance: I was thinking of visiting your country. What's the best month for a holiday there? ....
Acquaintance: Really? What's so good about that month? ....
Acquaintance: I see, mmm, it sounds nice.

End of exercise 3.

Exercise 4 Reacting to the unexpected

In this exercise we'd like you to give your own real opinions about a number of topics. Try to use a different way of introducing your opinion each time. Listen to an example first:

Reporter: What's your view of living in tall blocks of high-rise flats?
Model: I sometimes think that the planners made a big mistake when they started building these flats. People hate living in them.

OK? Now there are no model answers, so you will need to check your answers very carefully later when you listen to them afterwards. Right, now give your opinions. Imagine you are being interviewed by a radio reporter in the street.

Reporter: What's your opinion about high-rise flats? ....
Reporter: What do you think about the energy crisis? ....
Reporter: What's your view of the President of the United States? ....
Reporter: And how about the British Prime Minister, what's your opinion of the Prime Minister? ....
Reporter: And do you have any views on the leader of your own country? ....
Reporter: And what's your opinion of the school or college you're studying in at the moment? ....
Reporter: Something else I'd like to know is this: what do you think of the police force in this country? ....
Reporter: Oh and one last question: do you think there will *ever* be peace in the world? ....

That's the end of exercise 4.

Exercise 5 Participating in a conversation

In this exercise you are Pat and you are going to have to participate in the conversation. Listen first, your friends John and Mary are discussing ghosts and the supernatural.

John: I must say Mary, your belief in ghosts is totally irrational. Obviously there's no such thing.
Mary: Well, I'm not so sure. I know I've never seen one but there's enough evidence of other people seeing them for me to believe. I think ghosts do exist. Don't you, Pat?
....

Mary: Uhhu, I see. I don't mean, by the way, that they're necessarily frightening. If I saw a ghost I don't think I'd be frightened. Pat, what would you feel if you saw a ghost? ....

Right, now let's start again. This time you must state your opinion, agree or disagree when you are asked. There are no model answers in this exercise. You are Pat, remember. Ready?

John: I must say Mary, your belief in ghosts is totally irrationa[l] Obviously there's no such thing.

Mary: Well, I'm not so sure. I know I've never seen one but there's enough evidence of other people seeing them for me to believe. I think ghosts do exist. Don't you, Pat? ....

Mary: Uhhu, I see. I don't mean, by the way, that they're necessarily frightening. If I saw a ghost I don't think I'd be frightened. Pat, how would you feel if you saw a ghost? ....

John: Mmm. Well, as far as I'm concerned all this evidence of supernatural events is bogus. Don't you agree that it's al[l] bogus, Pat? ....

Mary: I'm afraid I don't quite understand the word 'bogus' John.

John: I mean all the evidence is faked, it's all false evidence. I mean the people who claim to have seen ghosts are all liars. Don't you agree, Pat? ....

Mary: Look John, I think you're exaggerating. Take the example of my grandmother. She told me about the time she was working as a servant before the war and the house she was working in was haunted. Anyway, there was the ghost of a young woman who walked through the house every night at midnight.

John: Huh. What's your opinion of that story, Pat? ....

John: Mary, you've been talking nonsense, really you have.

Mary: Not at all. That house I was talking about is still standin[g] It's on the corner of Wellington Road. It's up for sale *every* year. People move in, realize it's haunted and mov[e] out as quickly as possible. I mean who wants to live in a haunted house?

John: Sorry, what did Mary just say, Pat? I didn't quite follow. Which house was she talking about? ....

John: Oh, I see *that* house! Well I must say *I*'d have no fears about living in a so-called haunted house, would you Pat[?] ....

John: Your so-called ghosts are just the same as these UFOs.
Mary: UFOs?
John: Yes, these unidentified flying objects people keep claiming to have seen. Huh, flying saucers are impossible.
Mary: Let's see if Pat agrees. Pat, do you believe in UFOs?

....

Mary: Oh, I don't quite see what you mean Pat, could you put that another way? ....
Mary: I see. Well, John . . . [*knock, knock*] . . . yes?
Presenter: Sorry to interrupt but that's the end of exercise 5.
Mary and John: Oh, OK.

And for the communication activity have a look at your workbook and find a partner. Call your teacher, if you're working in a language laboratory.
End of unit 8.

In the communication activity, one student looks at activity K, while the other looks at activity B. Each has different ideas on how a mutual friend can get through an imminent exam. The activity practises giving opinions, agreeing and disagreeing.

Unit 9 Describing things, instructing people how to do things, checking understanding

The first two exercises in this unit are for you to listen to and draw a picture of the objects described. There's a space in your workbook for you to draw in. You need a pencil and perhaps a rubber for this.

Exercise 1 Before you start drawing it's probably best to listen to the whole description through once first. Then listen again and draw. Ready?

[*Description of an Anglepoise lamp*]
Hallo. I've just bought one of those amazing lamps that you can stand on the table and then point it in any direction that you like. You know the kind of thing I mean? It's got a round, flat, quite heavy base and then coming up from the base there's an arm. And it's usually got an elbow in it, you know, a bend, and so it's . . . so the arm's in two sections, and then at the end of that there's the shade and the bulb. Are you with me? You know, from the base there's always a spring of some sort so that

you can bend it right over if you want to, or you can have it standing straight up, and then at the elbow there's more springs so that you can have it going straight up to the ceiling or point it back down towards its own base. And the flex goes in through the base, up past the springs, up to the elbow, round the elbow and then down into the shade which has the lamp inside it. And there's one of those press-button switches on the top of the lamp. D'you know the kind of thing I mean?

End of exercise 1.

Exercise 2 Here's a description of the second object:

[*Description of a picnic table*]
This is a kind of table which is very useful in a garden, or at a picnic site, because the seating and the table surface are combined together into one piece of furniture. It's made of wood entirely and although it's quite heavy two people can move it around, put it where they like, follow the sun with it. Now, it's constructed in this way: there's the table surface which is about two metres long, is made up of several strips of wood – perhaps about ten centimetres wide – and these are screwed to a batten which runs underneath the table top. At each end the legs are attached to this batten as well. And the legs are made more or less in the shape of a capital letter A, although flattened a bit at the top where the . . . where they meet the table surface, so that the legs are wider at the base than they are at the table top. Where the bar goes across the middle of the capital letter A it's extended a bit on each side and this gives a projecting support. Now, the seating is attached to the ends of this bar so that they run along the side of the table joining the two legs. You have to climb into it to sit on it, but it provides seating for, say, three people on each side.

When you've drawn both objects, compare your drawing with a partner's drawings, if you can.
End of exercise 2.

Exercise 3 Giving spoken instructions

Look at your workbook. There is a set of instructions on how to serve yourself at a petrol station. These are in note form. In this exercise we'd like you to tell a stranger how to work the pump. Like this:

Stranger: Can you tell me how to use this pump?
Model: Yes, certainly. First of all, you have to press the red signal button to draw the cashier's attention.
Stranger: I see, then what?
Model: When you've done that, you have to take off the cap of your petrol tank.

OK, now it's your turn. The model answers are for guidance only, by the way. Start from the beginning again.

Stranger: Can you help me? I'd like to know how to work this pump. ....
Model: Yes, certainly. First of all, you have to press the red signal button to draw the cashier's attention.
Stranger: I see, then what? ....
Model: When you've done that, you have to take off the cap of your petrol tank.
Stranger: OK. Then? ....
Model: Then you select the grade of petrol you want: 2-star, 3-star or 4-star.
Stranger: Uhhu. I see. ....
Model: When you've done that you take the nozzle from its holster on the side of the pump.
Stranger: OK. ....
Model: And then you put the nozzle into your petrol tank.
Stranger: Fine. Alright. ....
Model: The next thing you do is squeeze the trigger and go on squeezing until you've got the amount of petrol you want. Or until it stops automatically.
Stranger: Sorry, but how do I know how much petrol I've got? ....
Model: Well, you just look at the indicator on the front of the pump.
Stranger: I see, sorry. What next? ....
Model: When you've got the petrol you want, you put the nozzle back in its holster.
Stranger: I see. OK. ....
Model: And then you must remember to put the cap back on your petrol tank.
Stranger: And that's it, is it? ....
Model: Just one more thing: check the price you have to pay on the indicator and pay the cashier.
Stranger: Fine. Well thanks very much for your help. That's all very clear now. ....
Model: Not at all, my pleasure.

End of exercise 3.

Exercise 4 Describing diagrams

Look at your workbook and describe each of the pictures there. Give a brief description of each, then listen to the model version for comparison. Like this:

Presenter: One
Model: There are two diagonal lines across the top left-hand corner and in the bottom right-hand corner there's a circle with a dot in the middle.

Right now give your own description of each picture. Ready?

Presenter: One ....
Model: There are two diagonal lines across the top left-hand corner and in the bottom right-hand corner there's a circle with a dot in the middle.

Presenter: Two ....
Model: There are two circles in the centre one above the other. The upper circle has a cross inside it and the lower circle has a tick inside it.

Presenter: Three ....
Model: There's a diagonal line across the bottom right-hand corner and there are marks along it at regular intervals, every fifth mark is longer than the others. It looks a bit like a ruler.

Presenter: Four ....
Model: Going up the centre there's a spiral with an arrow at the top pointing to the right. On the right there's a heavy line with an arrow pointing downwards.

Presenter: Five ....
Model: There's a diagonal zig-zag line going from the top left-hand corner towards the bottom. In the top right-hand corner there's a large dot.

Presenter: Six ....
Model: There are two oval shapes one inside the other in the centre. It looks a bit like a fried egg.

Presenter: Seven ....
Model: There's absolutely nothing in this picture, it's completely blank. It could be a snowstorm I suppose.

Presenter: Eight ....
Model: There are two lines going across the left-hand side and between the lines there are four patches. It looks a bit like a giraffe passing a window.

End of exercise 4.

Exercise 5 Instructing someone how to use this equipment

Before you begin, make notes on how to use this language laboratory booth or this cassette recorder. Stop the tape now and start it again when you're ready. If you're working at home, use a blank cassette for your recording. If you're in a language laboratory, let your teacher know when you're ready to start and when you've finished.
End of exercise 5.
There's a communication activity for you to do with a partner. Look at your workbook for the instructions. Call your teacher if you're working in a language laboratory.
End of unit 9.

In the communication activity, each student begins by drawing four diagrams. These have to be described to and drawn by the partner. Then each student draws four more diagrams.
Note that exercise 5 practises speaking freely. There is a key to exercises 1 and 2 in communication activity F.

Unit 10 Talking about similarities, talking about differences, stating preferences

Exercise 1 Talking about similarities

Listen to these examples first:

Friend: I can't decide whether to fly by Pan Am or British Airways to New York.
Model: Well, Pan Am and British Airways have a lot in common. For example, they both fly 747s to New York.

Friend: I can't make up my mind whether to get a Jaguar or a Rover.
Model: Well, there isn't much difference between a Jaguar and a Rover. For example, they're both made by British Leyland.

Now make similar comments in answer to your friend's remarks. Look at your workbook for some suggestions on how to reply. Ready?

Friend: I can't decide whether to fly by Pan Am or British Airways to New York. ....
Model: Well, Pan Am and British Airways have quite a lot in common. For example, they both fly Jumbo jets to New York.

Friend: I can't make up my mind whether to buy a Jaguar or a Rover. ....
Model: Well, there isn't much difference between a Jaguar and a Rover. For example, they're both made by British Leyland.

Friend: I can't tell the difference between an oak tree and a beech tree. ....
Model: Well, an oak tree and a beech tree have quite a lot in common. For example, they both lose their leaves in winter.

Friend: I can't make up my mind whether to buy a VW Golf or a Fiat Ritmo. ....
Model: Well, a Golf and a Ritmo are fairly similar. For example they're both hatchbacks. By the way the Ritmo's called a Strada in Britain. And a Golf's called a Rabbit in America.

Friend: I want to get a dog. The problem is which? I could either get an Alsatian or a Labrador. ....
Model: Well, an Alsatian and a Labrador have quite a lot in common. For example, they're both quite large dogs. By the way an Alsatian's called a German Shepherd in America.

Friend: Is that tree over there a pine tree or a fir tree? ....
Model: Well, there isn't much difference between a pine tree and a fir tree. For example, they're both evergreens.

Friend: I see, but what about that tree over there, which is it? ....
Model: I'm afraid I don't know, sorry.

End of exercise 1.

Exercise 2 Talking about similarities again

Look at your workbook and listen to these examples:

Friend: What's the difference between Henry and Michael?
Model: Well, there isn't much difference between Henry and Michael, actually. They're more or less the same height.
Friend: What about their personalities? Michael's much nicer than Henry.
Model: Ah yes! That's the main difference between them.

Friend: What's the difference between baby Zoë and baby Oliver?
Model: Well, baby Zoë and baby Oliver are fairly similar, actually. They're more or less the same weight.
Friend: What about their behaviour? Surely Zoë's much quieter than Oliver?
Model: Ah yes! That's the main difference between them.

Now follow the pattern and reply to the questions yourself. Ready?

Friend: What's the difference between Henry and Michael?
....
Model: Well, there isn't much difference between Henry and Michael, actually. They're both more or less the same height.
Friend: What about their personalities? Surely Michael's much more friendly than Henry? ....
Model: Ah yes! That's the main difference between them.

Friend: What's the difference between baby Zoë and baby Oliver? ....
Model: Well, baby Zoë and baby Oliver are fairly similar, actually. They're more or less the same weight.
Friend: What about their behaviour? Surely Zoë's less noisy than Oliver? ....
Model: Ah yes! That's the main difference between them.

Friend: I gather that the Netherlands and Belgium are quite similar. ....
Model: Yes, there isn't much difference between the Netherlands and Belgium, actually. They're more or less the same size.
Friend: Yes, but don't half the Belgians speak French, not Dutch? ....
Model: Ah yes! That's the main difference between them.

Friend: I'm thinking of buying a new car. Perhaps a Ford Fiest or a Peugeot 104. ....
Model: Well, a Ford Fiesta and a Peugeot 104 have quite a lot in common, actually. They're more or less the same price.
Friend: Yes, but hasn't a Peugeot got five doors, not just three? ....
Model: Ah yes! That's the main difference between them.

Friend: Can you tell the difference between butter and margarine? ....
Model: Well, there isn't much difference between butter and margarine, actually. They're both more or less the same colour, texture and taste.
Friend: Yes, but what about the price? ....
Model: Ah yes! That's the main difference between them.
Friend: Hmm. I don't agree they *taste* the same, you know. ....
Model: Well, they do to me.

End of exercise 2.

Exercise 3 Pointing out differences

Listen carefully to these examples:

Friend: Isn't the population of London 28 million?
Model: Oh no, it's nowhere near as large as that.
Friend: Really?
Model: Mmm, as far as I know, it's about a quarter the size you said.

Friend: Isn't the River Thames 1200 kilometres long?
Model: Oh no, it's nothing like as long as that.
Friend: Really?
Model: Mmm, as far as I know, it's about a quarter the length you said.

Now answer the questions yourself. The figures given are all *four* times too big. Ready?

Friend: Isn't the population of London 28 million? ....
Model: Oh no, it's nowhere near as large as that.
Friend: Really? ....
Model: Mmm, as far as I know, it's about a quarter the size you said.

Friend: Isn't the River Thames 1200 kilometres long? ....
Model: Oh no, it's nothing like as long as that.
Friend: Really? ....
Model: Mmm, as far as I know, it's about a quarter the length you said.

Friend: Isn't the English Channel 120 kilometres wide at Dover? ....
Model: Oh no, it's nowhere near as wide as that.
Friend: Really? ....
Model: Mmm, as far as I know it's about a quarter the width you said.

Friend: Isn't the Tower of London 4000 years old? ....
Model: Oh no, it's nothing like as old as that.
Friend: Are you sure? ....
Model: Mmm, as far as I know it's about a quarter the age you said.

Friend: Isn't Mount Everest 35,000 metres high? ....
Model: Oh no, it's nothing like as high as that.
Friend: Really? ....
Model: Mmm, as far as I know it's about a quarter the height you said.

Friend: Isn't the deepest part of the Pacific Ocean 40 kilometres deep? ....
Model: Oh no, it's nowhere near as deep as that.
Friend: Really? ....
Model: Mmm, as far as I know it's about a quarter the depth you said.
Friend: What? 10 kilometres deep? ....
Model: That's right.
Friend: Mmm. That's still very deep isn't it?
Model: Yes.

End of exercise 3.

Exercise 4 Stating preferences and giving reasons

Look at the examples in your workbook and listen carefully.

Friend: We could have grilled trout or we could make a rabbit stew.
Model: I'd much prefer to have trout because it'd be so much easier to cook.

Friend: We could hire a Ford Escort or a Range Rover.
Model: I'd much rather hire an Escort because it'd be so muc easier to drive.

Now tell your friend which of the things he suggests *you* prefe and why. Ready? As usual, the model answers are for guidance only.

Friend: We could have grilled trout or we could make a rabbit stew. ....
Model: I'd much prefer to have trout because it'd be so much easier to cook.

Friend: We could hire an Escort or a Range Rover. ....
Model: I'd much rather hire an Escort because it'd be so much easier to drive.

Friend: I think we've learnt enough English, shall we start learning Italian or Chinese now? ....
Model: I'd much prefer to start learning Italian because it'd be so much easier to understand.

Friend: We could see the news on TV or hear it on the radio. ....
Model: I'd much rather see it on TV because it'd be so much easier to follow.

Friend: You could put on jeans or a suit. ....
Model: I'd much prefer to put on jeans because they'd be so much more comfortable to wear.

Friend: You could buy an Instamatic camera or an expensive single-lens reflex. ....
Model: I'd much prefer to buy an Instamatic because it'd be so much easier to use.

Friend: You could have a cat or you could have a dog as a pet. ....
Model: I'd much rather have a cat because it'd be so much easier to look after.

Friend: You could go on a donkey or a camel. ....
Model: I'd much prefer to go on a donkey because it'd be so much easier to ride.
Friend: Yes, riding a camel's really difficult – and uncomfortable, too!

End of exercise 4.

Exercise 5 Talking about similarities and differences

In this exercise you're going to be asked a series of questions. The model answers are for guidance only. Listen to one example first.

Friend: What's the difference between a chair and a stool?
Model: Well, you can sit on them both, but the main difference is that a stool doesn't have a back and you can't lean back on it.

OK. Now, it's your turn.

Friend: What's the difference between a chair and a stool. ....
Model: Well, you can sit on them both, but the main difference is that a stool doesn't have a back – you can't lean back on it.

Friend: What's the difference between a moped and a motorcycle? ....
Model: Well, you can ride them both, but the main difference is that a moped is much less powerful than a motorcycle – and it has pedals like a bicycle, too.

Friend: What's the difference between a lesson and a lecture? ....
Model: Well, they're both ways of giving knowledge, but the main difference is that you participate in a lesson whereas you just listen to a lecture. A lecture's generally given to a much larger group.

Friend: What's the difference between a desk and a table? ....
Model: Well, they're both things you can sit at, but the main difference is that a desk is usually used for work and a table for eating. A desk generally has drawers, too.

Friend: What's the difference between a tree and a bush? ....
Model: Well, they're both things that grow, but the main difference is that a tree is much taller than a bush. A bush often has leaves all the way down to the ground, too.

Friend: What's the difference between a gate and a door? ....
Model: Well, they're both things you can open and close, but the main difference is that a door is generally found in a building, whereas a gate is usually found outside.

Friend: What's the difference between a fence and a wall? ....
Model: Well, they're both things that can divide one garden from another, but the main difference is that a fence made of wood or metal whereas a wall is made of bri[illegible] or stone.

Friend: What's the difference between a rug and a carpet? ....
Model: Well, they're both things you put on the floor, but th[illegible] main difference is that a rug's much smaller than a ca[illegible]pet. In fact, you can put a rug over part of a carpet.

Friend: One last question: what's the difference between an encyclopedia and a dictionary? ....
Model: Well, they're both reference books, but the main diffe[illegible]ence is that you look up information in an encyclope[illegible] and you look up the meaning of words in a dictionary[illegible] And a dictionary generally explains how to pronounc[illegible] words, too.
Friend: Fine. That's all. Thanks.

End of exercise 5.
There is a communication activity, for which you need to find [illegible] partner. The instructions are printed in your workbook.
End of unit 10.

In the communication activity, one student looks at activity H, while the other looks at activity D. One has information about the Cambridge First Certificate exam, the other about the ARELS Certificate exam. They discuss the differences and similarities.

Unit 11 Making suggestions and giving advice, expressing enthusiasm, persuading

Exercise 1 Offering sympathetic advice

Cassette 3 Side 1

In this exercise a friend is going to ask you for some advice. Suggest what you think he should do. Listen to these examples first:

Friend: Oh dear! I've got a bit of a headache.
Model: In that case perhaps you'd better take something for it.

Friend: Oh dear! This pen won't write.
Model: In that case perhaps it'd be a good idea to use a pencil.

Now, follow the pattern and offer advice yourself. Imagine you are talking to a friend.

Friend: Oh dear! I've got a bit of a headache. ....
Model: In that case perhaps you'd better take something for it.

Friend: Oh dear! My pen won't work. ....
Model: In that case perhaps it'd be a good idea to use a pencil.

Friend: Ugh! This coffee isn't sweet enough. ....
Model: In that case perhaps you'd better put some more sugar in it.

Friend: Oh dear, I don't know what this word means. ....
Model: In that case it might be an idea to look it up in a dictionary.

Friend: Oh, it's getting very dark in here. I can't see properly. ....
Model: In that case perhaps you'd better put the light on.

Friend: My car's been making some very strange noises. ....
Model: In that case perhaps it'd be a good idea to take it to a garage.

Friend: I've got a bit of a pain in my back. I don't know what to do. ....
Model: In that case perhaps you'd better go to the doctor's.

Friend: Oh dear, my throat's ever so dry ....
Model: In that case perhaps you ought to have something to drink.

End of exercise 1.

Exercise 2 Advising an acquaintance on more serious problems

This time an acquaintance has some rather more difficult problems to solve. Listen to these examples first:

Acquaintance: I wish I could stop smoking.
Model: Hmm, that's quite a problem. Have you ever thought of trying to cut down gradually?
Acquaintance: That's a good idea.

Acquaintance: I always seem to fail every exam I take.
Model: Hmm, that's quite a problem. Might it be an idea to try to revise systematically?
Acquaintance: Yes, I ought to try that.

Now it's your turn to make the suggestions. The model answers are for guidance only. Imagine you're talking to an acquaintanc

Acquaintance: I wish I could give up smoking. ....
Model: Hmm, that's quite a problem. Have you ever thought of trying to cut down gradually?
Acquaintance: That's easier said than done.

Acquaintance: I always seem to fail every exam I take. ....
Model: Hmm, that's quite a problem. Might it be an idea to try to revise systematically?
Acquaintance: Yes, it's a question of getting organized, I suppose.

Acquaintance: Oh dear, I just seem to be putting on more and more weight these days. ....
Model: Hmm, that's quite a problem. Have you ever thought of trying to eat less?
Acquaintance: I've tried – I just can't stop eating.

Acquaintance: Whenever I go for an interview I seem to make a bad impression. I don't know if it's my clothes? ....
Model: Hmm, that's quite a problem. Have you ever thought of trying to dress more smartly?
Acquaintance: Yes, perhaps I ought to buy a suit.

Acquaintance: Oh dear, I wish I had more money left at the end of the month. I'm broke again. ....
Model: Hmm, that's quite a problem. Don't you think it might be an idea to try to spend less and save a bit each month?
Acquaintance: That's easier said than done.

Acquaintance: Whenever I talk to people I seem to upset them. What can I do? ....
Model: Hmm, that's quite a problem. Have you ever thought of trying to speak more politely?
Acquaintance: What do you mean 'more politely'?

Acquaintance: Ohh! I feel so lonely sitting at home by myself every evening. ....
Model: Hmm, that's quite a problem. Might it be an idea to try to meet more people?
Acquaintance: Yes, I really ought to start going out more.

Acquaintance: Oh dear, I've got a terrible memory. I keep forgetting that I've arranged to meet people. ....
Model: Hmm, that's quite a problem. Don't you think it might be an idea to try to keep an engagement diary?
Acquaintance: What a good idea! Thanks for the advice.

End of exercise 2.

Exercise 3 Making enthusiastic suggestions to a friend

Look at your workbook and listen to these examples:

Friend: Ohh! I don't know what to do on Monday.
Model: Hey listen, this'd be great! Why don't you and I go to the cinema together?
Friend: Alright!

Friend: I don't know what to do on Tuesday.
Model: Hey listen, I think it'd be a great idea if you and I had dinner together!
Friend: That'd be nice!

Now make the enthusiastic suggestions yourself. Imagine you're talking to a friend. Ready?

Friend: I don't know what to do on Monday. ....
Model: Hey listen, this'd be great! Why don't you and I go to the cinema together?
Friend: Alright!

Friend: I don't know what I'm going to do on Tuesday evening. ....
Model: Hey listen, I think it'd be a great idea if you and I had dinner together!
Friend: That'd be nice!

Friend: Wednesday's going to be a boring evening. ....
Model: Hey listen, I've got a great idea! Why don't you and I go to the concert together?
Friend: Oh, yes, I'd enjoy that!

Friend: I've got nothing planned for Thursday. ....
Model: Hey listen, I think it'd be a great idea if you and I went sailing together!
Friend: Mmm! Thanks!

Friend: I'm always at a loose end on Fridays. ....
Model: Hey listen, I've got a great idea! Why don't you and I go for a walk together?
Friend: I'm afraid I can't, I've hurt my foot.

Friend: Next weekend's going to be really dull after such a busy week. I've got nothing on at all. ....
Model: Hey listen, I think it'd be a fantastic idea if we both went to Bournemouth for the weekend!
Friend: Bournemouth? What could we do there? ....
Model: Well, we could go swimming, see the shops, have a mea stay in a smart hotel, see a . . .

End of exercise 3.

Exercise 4 Rejecting a friend's advice

Look at your workbook and listen to these examples:

Friend: Now, you want to improve your English. If I were you I'd study for four hours every night.
Model: That's easier said than done, you see I haven't got that much time to spare.

Friend: And it'd be a good idea to read at least two English newspapers every day.
Model: That's all very well, but I can't afford to buy two newspapers a day.

Now state your reservations or objections to the suggestions. Use your own ideas – the model answers are for guidance only. Ready?

Friend: Now, I've got some advice for you if you want to improve your English. First of all, you ought to study for four hours every evening. ....
Model: That's easier said than done, you see I haven't got that much time to spare.

Friend: And it'd be a good idea to read at least two English newspapers every day. ....
Model: That's all very well, but I can't afford to buy two newspapers a day.

Friend: Have you ever thought of watching BBC TV every evening? ....
Model: That's easier said than done, you see I can't get BBC TV programmes in my country.

Friend: Might it be an idea to read your grammar book through chapter by chapter? ....
Model: That's all very well, but it's a bit boring to read about grammar, isn't it?

Friend: Hey listen, this'd be great! Why don't you talk to your brothers and sisters in English? ....
Model: That's easier said than done, you see they wouldn't understand me.

Friend: I know what you could do. You could learn fifty new words every day. ....
Model: That's all very well, but I'm afraid I'd forget them.

Friend: Look, why don't you give up learning English altogether and take up another language? ....
Model: That's easier said than done, you see I think any other language would be even more difficult than English.

End of exercise 4.

Exercise 5 Offering helpful suggestions and advice to a friend

In this exercise there are no model answers. Imagine you're talking to a friend and offer helpful advice or suggestions. Here's one example:

Friend: What can I do? I've got terrible toothache.
Model: Oh dear, I'm sorry to hear that. If I were you I'd make an appointment with the dentist.

OK. Now it's your turn.

Friend: What can I do? I've got an awful headache. ....
Friend: (sneeze) I feel terrible today. What do you think I should do? ....
Friend: I'm ever so hungry, but I can't afford to buy any lunch. ....
Friend: My cat's ill I think. She won't eat anything and she's getting thinner and thinner. ....
Friend: Do you know a good book I could read? ....
Friend: I've lost my purse. I think it's been stolen! ....

Friend: I've got a hole in the elbow of my pullover. ....

Friend: Every time I drink wine I get a headache the next day. ....

Friend: I don't know what to do. I think my English is getting worse. I've been studying hard for six months and I don't think I'm making any progress. ....

End of exercise 5.
Now there is a communication activity, for which you need to find a partner. The instructions are printed in your workbook.
End of unit 11.

In the communication activity, one student looks at activity Y, while the other looks at activity S. Each has information about Dorchester in Dorset, where they have decided to spend a day together. The idea is to persuade each other to accept the plans each of them has.

Unit 12 Complaining, apologizing and forgiving, expressing disappointment

Exercise 1 Apologetic responses

In this exercise you're going to apologize for various things you've done wrong. Look at your workbook and listen to these examples:

Landlady: I'm sorry to bring this up, but you haven't paid me for the dry-cleaning I had done for you.

Model: Oh dear, I'm most awfully sorry, Mrs Rogers. Here you are.

Landlord: I'm sorry to have to say this but you keep arriving late for dinner. I find it very annoying.

Model: I'm so sorry, Mr Rogers. I didn't realize. I'll be on time tomorrow.

Now it's your turn to apologize. Imagine you're talking to the landlady and landlord in the English family you're staying with – they are called Mr and Mrs Rogers. Try to use a different apologetic response each time. The model answers are for guidance only. Ready?

Landlady: I'm sorry to bring this up, but you haven't paid me for the dry-cleaning I had done for you. ....

Model: Oh dear, I'm most awfully sorry, Mrs Rogers. Here you are.

Landlord: I'm sorry to have to say this, but you keep arriving late for dinner. I find it very annoying. ....

Model: I'm so sorry, Mr Rogers. I didn't realize. I'll make sure I'm on time tomorrow.

Landlord: I'm sorry to have to say this but you're sitting in my chair again. ....

Model: I'm ever so sorry, Mr Rogers. I didn't realize it was *your* chair. I'll go and sit over there.

Landlady: Look, I'm sorry to bring this up, but you forgot to lock the front door this morning. Anyone could have walked in! ....

Model: Oh dear, I'm ever so sorry, Mrs Rogers. It won't happen again.

Landlord: I'm sorry to disturb you while you're studying, but you left the tap running in the bathroom. The whole room is flooded. ....

Model: Oh, I just don't know what to say Mr Rogers. Let me help you to mop it up.

Landlady: Look, I'm sorry to have to say this, but if you want to make a phone call you *must* ask permission first. ....

Model: I'm most awfully sorry, Mrs Rogers. Normally I would, but it was rather urgent.

Landlady: Thank you so much for doing the washing-up last night, just one little thing though: do you think you could rinse the plates next time? ....

Model: Oh, I'm ever so sorry, Mrs Rogers. Yes, of course I will.

Landlord: Oh, and one last thing: you didn't turn off the lights when you came in last night. ....

Model: Didn't I? Oh I'm dreadfully sorry, Mr Rogers. I'll make sure I do next time.

Landlord: Yes, please do.

End of exercise 1.

Exercise 2 Complaining

In this exercise you're the Head of Department in a language school – your name is Mr Jones, and you're telling members of your teaching staff that you're dissatisfied with certain aspects of their work. Look at your workbook and listen to the examples:

Mr Roberts: You wanted to see me, Mr Jones.
Model: Yes, Mr Roberts, I'm sorry to have to say this, but you were late again this morning.
Mr Roberts: Oh dear, I'm very sorry. My alarm clock didn't go off.
Model: I see, well, please make sure you get here on time in future, alright?
Mr Roberts: Of course, yes, I'm sorry.

Mr Forster: You wanted to see me, Mr Jones.
Model: Yes, Mr Forster, I'm sorry to bring this up, but you've been telling too many jokes in class.
Mr Forster: Oh dear, look, I'm very sorry, but the class seem to like my little jokes.
Model: I see, well, please make sure your lessons are more serious in future, alright?
Mr Forster: Of course, yes, I'm sorry.

Now it's your turn to play the part of the Head of Department and complain to your staff. Ready? Start with Mr Roberts.

Mr Roberts: You wanted to see me, Mr Jones. ....
Model: Yes, Mr Roberts, I'm sorry to have to say this, but you were late again this morning.
Mr Roberts: Oh dear, I'm very sorry. My alarm clock didn't go off. ....
Model: I see, well, please make sure you get here on time in future, alright?
Mr Roberts: Of course, yes, I'm sorry.

Mr Forster: You wanted to see me, Mr Jones. ....
Model: Yes, Mr Forster, I'm sorry to bring this up, but you've been telling too many jokes in class.
Mr Forster: Oh dear, look I'm very sorry, but the class seem to like my little jokes. ....
Model: I see, well, please make sure your lessons are more serious in future, alright?
Mr Forster: Of course, yes, I'm sorry.

Miss Robinson: You wanted to see me, Mr Jones. ....
Model: Yes, Miss Robinson, I'm sorry to have to say this, but you haven't set your class any homework this month.
Miss Robinson: Oh dear, I'm very sorry, but they don't seem to like doing homework. ....
Model: I see, well, please make sure you set them homework regularly in future, alright?
Miss Robinson: I'll try, I'm sorry.

Mr Shave: You wanted to see me, Mr Jones. ....
Model: Yes, Mr Shave, I'm sorry to bring this up, but you've been going too fast with class A2.
Mr Shave: Oh dear, have I? But they seem to like going fast. ....
Model: I see, well, please make sure you go more slowly in future, alright?
Mr Shave: Oh yes, I will. Sorry again.

Ms Geller: You wanted to see me, Mr Jones. ....
Model: Yes, Ms Geller, I'm sorry to have to say this, but you didn't prepare your lessons today.
Ms Geller: Oh dear, I'm very sorry. I didn't have time. I had a lot of homework to mark. ....
Model: I see, well, please make sure you prepare your lessons in future, alright?
Ms Geller: Of course, yes, I'm very sorry.

Mr Goodman: You wanted to see me, Mr Jones. ....
Model: Yes, Mr Goodman, I'm sorry to bring this up, but I've heard the lecture you gave yesterday was rather boring.
Mr Goodman: Oh dear, I'm very sorry. You see the subject matter of the lecture was rather theoretical. ....
Model: I see, well, please make sure your lectures are more interesting in future, alright?
Mr Goodman: Er, yes of course, I'll make a special effort. Is that all, Mr Jones? ....
Model: Yes, thanks.

End of exercise 2.

Exercise 3 Forgiving

In this exercise, various people are going to apologize to you. You should forgive them. Listen to these examples:

Acquaintance: I'm not quite sure how to put this, but I've just drunk your tea by mistake.
Model: Oh, that's alright, don't worry.

Friend: I'm afraid I've got something to tell you: I've forgotten to post that letter you gave me.
Model: Oh, never mind, it doesn't really matter.

Now it's your turn to forgive. Try to use a different expression each time. Ready?

Acquaintance: I'm not quite sure how to put this, but I've just drunk your tea by mistake. ....
Model: Oh, that's alright, don't worry.

Friend: I'm afraid I've got something to tell you: I've forgotten to post that letter you gave me. ....
Model: Oh, never mind, it doesn't really matter.

Acquaintance: I've got a bit of an apology to make, you see I managed to get *myself* a ticket, but it was the last one, so there isn't one for you. Sorry. ....
Model: Oh, never mind, it's not your fault.

Friend: Look, I'm ever so sorry, but you can't come with us to the beach. There isn't any room in the car. ....
Model: Oh well, never mind. It doesn't really matter. It's probably going to rain anyway.

Acquaintance: Sorry to have to tell you this, but you know the book you lent me, well, somebody's walked off with it. Sorry. ....
Model: Oh, please don't blame yourself, I can always buy another copy.

Friend: Um, this isn't easy to explain, but you know I promised to tell you when Sandy was coming round? Well, I forgot and now it's too late. ....
Model: Oh, that's alright. I can see Sandy some other time.

Acquaintance: I'm not quite sure how to put this, but I seem to have broken your watch. Terribly sorry.

....

Model: Oh, never mind, it doesn't really matter. It didn't keep good time anyway. I can buy myself a new one now!

Presenter: Look, this isn't easy to explain, but I'm afraid we're just coming to the end of this exercise. Awfully sorry. ....

Model: Oh, that's alright, I've had enough anyway.

End of exercise 3.

Exercise 4 Apologizing and making excuses

In this exercise you are Jo and you have to telephone various friends to apologize for things you have done or not done. Look at your workbook and listen to the examples:

Caroline: 249618.
Model: Hallo. Can I speak to Caroline, please?
Caroline: Speaking.
Model: Oh, hallo, Caroline. This is Jo. I'm terribly sorry I didn't manage to make it to your party last night.
Caroline: Yes, where were you? We were expecting you.
Model: Well, it's like this you see: my sister arrived unexpectedly at the airport and I had to go and meet her.
Caroline: Oh, I see. Well, never mind.

Jerry: 518924.
Model: Hallo. Can I speak to Jerry, please?
Jerry: Speaking.
Model: Oh, hallo, Jerry. This is Jo. I'm terribly sorry I didn't ring you yesterday.
Jerry: Yes, what happened? I was expecting you to call.
Model: Well, it's like this you see: I was very busy at work and I completely forgot to phone.
Jerry: Oh, I see. Well, not to worry.

Now it's your turn to phone each of your friends. Begin with Caroline.

Caroline: 249618. ....
Model: Hallo. Can I speak to Caroline, please?
Caroline: Speaking. ....
Model: Oh, hallo, Caroline. This is Jo. I'm terribly sorry I didn't manage to make it to your party last night.
Caroline: Yes, where *were* you? We were expecting you. ....
Model: Well, it's like this you see: my sister arrived unexpectedly at the airport and I had to go and meet he
Caroline: Oh, I see. Well, never mind.

Jerry: 518924. ....
Model: Hallo. Can I speak to Jerry, please?
Jerry: Speaking. ....
Model: Oh, hallo, Jerry. This is Jo. I'm terribly sorry I didn't ring you yesterday.
Jerry: Yes, what happened? I was expecting you to call. ....
Model: Well, it's like this you see: I was very busy at work and I completely forgot to phone.
Jerry: Oh, I see. Well, not to worry.

Alan: 114224. ....
Model: Hallo. Can I speak to Alan, please?
Alan: Speaking. ....
Model: Oh, hallo, Alan. This is Jo. I'm terribly sorry I didn't manage to get to the football match yesterday.
Alan: Yes, where were you? We had to play with ten men. ....
Model: Well, it's like this you see: I fell off my bicycle and sprained my ankle.
Alan: Oh dear. Well, get well soon!

Jan: 767294. ....
Model: Hallo. Can I speak to Jan, please?
Jan: Speaking. ....
Model: Oh, hallo, Jan. This is Jo. I'm terribly sorry I didn't manage to come round to your flat yesterday.
Jan: Yes, where were you? You could at least have phoned! ....
Model: Well, it's like this you see: I was in London but there was a strike on the railway and I couldn't find a phone box that worked.
Jan: I still think it's a bit much! I prepared a meal specially for you! ....
Model: Oh dear. Well, I'm most awfully sorry.
Jan: It couldn't be helped I suppose.

Man: 595951. ....
Model: Hallo. Can I speak to Desmond, please?
Man: Who do you want to speak to? ....
Model: Desmond.
Man: There's no Desmond here. What number did you want? ....
Model: 595591.
Man: This is 595951. ....
Model: Oh dear, I've got the wrong number. I'm sorry to have disturbed you.
Man: That's alright, goodbye.

Model: Oh well, try again!
Woman: 595591. ....
Model: Hallo. Can I speak to Desmond, please?
Woman: I'm afraid he's out. Can I take a message? ....
Model: My name's Jo. Could you tell him I'm terribly sorry, but I didn't manage to get any seats for the concert tonight.
Woman: OK. Shall I tell him anything else? ....
Model: Well, could you also tell him that the concert was fully booked and I'll phone him tomorrow.
Woman: Certainly. Goodbye! ....
Model: Goodbye!

End of exercise 4.

Exercise 5 Showing disappointment

In this exercise you're going to hear some bad news. You have to react with a suitably disappointed response. Listen first.

Friend 1: I've got a message from Rob: he's broken his arm so he can't play tennis with us this afternoon.
Model: Oh dear, I was really looking forward to playing tennis.
Friend 1: Still, it can't be helped. We can find someone else to play with us.

Friend 2: I'm afraid we can't go for a drive in the country. My car's broken down.
Model: Oh dear, it really is a shame that we can't go.
Friend 2: Oh well, not to worry. We'll find something else to do.

Now it's your turn to show your disappointment. Ready?

Friend 1: I've got a message from Rob: he's broken his arm so he can't play tennis with us this afternoon. ....
Model: Oh dear, I was really looking forward to playing tennis.
Friend 1: Still, it can't be helped. We can find someone else to play with us.

Friend 2: I'm afraid we can't go for a drive in the country. My car's broken down. ....
Model: Oh dear, it really is a shame that we can't go.
Friend 2: Oh well, not to worry. We'll find something else to do.

Friend 1: I've got some bad news I'm afraid. We've both failed that exam we took. ....
Model: Oh dear, what a shame! Still, *I* didn't expect to pass anyway.
Friend 1: No, you can't win them all. We can resit it next year, can't we?

Friend 2: It's just started to rain. That means our walk in the country's off now. ....
Model: Oh dear, I was really looking forward to going for a walk.
Friend 2: Still, we can go next weekend if the weather's nice.

Friend 1: You know that book I was going to lend you? Well, I'm afraid it fell in the bath so I had to throw it away. ....
Model: Oh dear, that really is a shame. I was looking forward to reading it, too.
Friend 1: Still, it's no good crying over spilt milk. You can buy your own copy now, can't you?

Friend 2: Well, that's it. We can't go to the theatre now. My parents are coming for the weekend. ....
Model: Oh dear, if only they'd told us earlier. We could have booked *them* tickets, too.
Friend 2: Still, it can't be helped. We could always ring up to see if there are any seats left, couldn't we?

Friend 1: Didn't I tell you? Our teacher's ill so there won't be a lesson today. ....
Model: Oh dear, I wish I'd known! I needn't have come to school.
Friend 1: Oh, not to worry. We can all go and have coffee together.

Friend 2: Oh, your sister phoned from Canada. She says she's not coming to visit you next week. ....
Model: Oh dear, I was really looking forward to seeing her.
Friend 2: Mm, but the good news is that she's coming the week after. ....
Model: Oh good, it'll be really nice to see her again after so long.

End of exercise 5.
There is a communication activity, for which you will need to find a partner. The instructions are printed in your workbook.
End of unit 12.

In the communication activity, one student looks at activity P, while the other looks at activity V. Each has two complaints and two apologies to make to the other.

Unit 13 Describing places, describing people

Exercise 1 You're going to hear a description of a scene. Look at your workbook for exercise 1. As you can see the scene is partly drawn already, but you'll have to fill in the details after you've heard the description. It's probably best to draw nothing until you've heard the whole description through. Then use a pencil, rather than a pen to draw your sketch. Ready?

[*Description of Leo, the MGM lion, in 1928*]
Well, in this picture there are two men on the right-hand side. One is standing and one is sitting in a folding chair. Now, the man in the folding chair is wearing a large, baggy cloth cap, a shirt, plus-fours – which are baggy, knee-length trousers which are tucked into woollen socks – and his trousers are held up by a thick leather belt and he's got a pair of headphones on. In front of him is a table with what appears to be some sort of recording equipment, and with his left hand he's twiddling one of the knobs. Behind the table there's a stand with a very old-fashioned microphone at the top. The microphone comes up to about the level of the head of the man who's standing. The man who's standing has got, er, again, got a cloth cap on, collar and tie, and a pullover, and just in front of him he's got an old-fashioned movie camera on a tripod. There are two reels on the top of the camera. The background of the picture appears to be a large curtain of some sort, but on the very right-hand side it's

drawn back a bit and you can just see that there are some bars. It appears that the whole picture is taken inside a cage of some sort. In front of the table that the sound-recordist has, are two boxes or stands which are made of wooden slats, and on top of these, with its hind feet on the slightly lower rear box, is a large lion who's standing with his mouth open. The camera's pointing directly into his face and the lion appears to be about to say something into the microphone, though I'm not quite sure what.

When you've finished your drawing, compare it with your neighbour's sketch, if you can. End of exercise 1.

Exercise 2 Here's another description of a scene, but a rather different one this time. Again listen to the whole description through once before you begin your drawing. Ready?

[*Description of the capsized* Normandie *in 1942*]
This is a scene of a water front and at the front of the picture running from left to right is a main road by the side of a river with a lot of traffic on it. They are old-fashioned, they look sort of nineteen-thirtyish saloon cars. It's obviously not in England because the cars are driving on the right-hand side of the road. At the back of the picture on the other side of the river it's very smoky, possibly foggy. There are a couple of smaller ships in the river. And the central point of the picture is this enormous liner which has capsized – it's lying on its side. Er . . . the bow of the liner is facing us as we look at the picture and the funnels are pointing to the right and it looks as if the ship has been on fire. Um, there's a smaller tug or fire ship which has hoses playing water onto the deck of the liner. Um, on the right-hand side of the picture there's a wharf or warehouse. It's a very nineteen-thirties design-style on the façade of the building, and the title of the liner company is written in letters, large letters, on the wall: CUNARD.

When you've finished your drawing, compare it with your neighbour's drawing, if you can. End of exercise 2.

Exercise 3 Look at your workbook. There are two rather similar pictures. Listen very carefully to this description of *one* of them and decide which one is being described.

[*Description of second picture*]
This is a picture of an old town on the other side of a river. Um, in the foreground there's this bank of the river, and then the river, and on the other side the town is just, um, built not quite up to the edge of the bank because there's grass between the river and the town itself. The buildings of the town are very square and very, um, very sort of geometrical in design and they are all packed very closely together. You have the impression that the streets of the town are very narrow, and er . . . sort of narrow streets between these high buildings. Um, there's a church in the town, there are two churches I can see in fact. Um, and there's quite a lot of greenery everywhere, there are trees scattered between the buildings especially higher up the slopes. Um, and the thing that strikes you most about the picture, I suppose, is the castle. There's a castle, um, above the other buildings in the town, and it's much higher up the hill than most of the other buildings. It dominates the town. And the river itself is flowing fairly smoothly along and there are . . . yes, I can see two men in a boat rowing along. And, erm, right in the front of the picture there's . . . there are trees and little bushes along the bank.

Have you decided which one? ....
Yes, it was the second picture. But how do you know? ....
Because the man mentioned the two men in a boat and the castle dominating the town and the bushes on the bank. End of exercise 3.

Exercise 4 Describing a place

Cassette 3 Side 2

Look at your workbook and answer these questions about the picture and the information. Imagine you're talking to a friend who wants to know about the place, because she's thinking of going there herself. Listen to one example first:

Friend: Where exactly is Rye?
Model: It's in Sussex in the south-east of England – about 90 kilometres from London.

Now answer the questions yourself. The model answers are for guidance only, by the way.

Friend: Where exactly is Rye? ....
Model: It's in Sussex in the south-east of England – about 90 kilometres from London.

Friend: And is it on the coast? ....
Model: Not exactly, but it used to be in the Middle Ages.

Friend: Is it a large modern city? ....
Model: Oh no, it's a small old town with narrow streets and historic buildings.

Friend: Is there much traffic in the centre of the town? ....
Model: Oh no, the streets are cobbled and you can walk along them without worrying about getting run over.

Friend: And what are the buildings like? ....
Model: As I said, they're very old, made of brick and wood and they're all built in different styles.

Friend: What hotels can you stay at? ....
Model: Well, there are two possibilities: the Hope Anchor Hotel and the Mermaid Inn.

Friend: Which would *you* recommend? ....
Model: Well, I think the Mermaid Inn would be marvellous – it's a really old building with four-poster beds in the bedrooms and a very friendly atmosphere.

Friend: Sounds terrific! It must be very popular? ....
Model: Yes, it says here that there are a lot of American tourists there so you'd certainly need to book ahead.

Friend: There must be some nice pubs in Rye? ....
Model: Yes, apart from the Mermaid itself, there's the Union in East Street and the Ypres Castle.

Friend: Which would be nicest on a warm summer evening? ....

Model: Oh, without doubt the Ypres Castle – it's got a big garden with views over the marshes to the sea in the distance.

Friend: And can you recommend a nice place for tea? ....
Model: Yes, there's a restaurant called Simon the Pieman which is supposed to be very nice.
Friend: OK, thanks very much.

End of exercise 4.

Exercise 5 In this exercise you're going to have to draw again. Look at your workbook. As you can see the outline of a group of people is shown – you have to fill in the details. Listen to the whole description through once before you start drawing. Use a pencil rather than a pen.

[*Description of a restaurant scene*]
This picture seems to be of a restaurant where meals are in progress. The background of the picture shows several tables, waiters rushing around. It's rather blurred, er, the most prominent waiter is one in the top right-hand corner. Er, there's a group of . . . er, they appear to be businessmen sitting at a table in the rear. Er, at the table in the foreground of the picture there are six people seated around it: two on the left-hand edge of the picture, three on the right-hand side of the picture and a gentleman sitting at the head of the table. The two people on the left-hand side are both wearing spectacles, um, neither of them is eating at the moment. The woman on the extreme edge of the picture seems to be talking intently, she's turning to the man on her left. The three people on the right-hand side of the picture, well, the one closest to the foreground is very blurred. He appears to have grey hair, but you . . . one can't really see much more about him. Er, next in line is a man with his hair brushed back off his forehead. He's eating what appears to be his dessert, he's got a spoon and a fork in his hand which he's holding rather delicately and he's concentrating on what he's eating. And next to him is a woman with a rather superior expression on her face, her eyes are partly closed, she's got short hair, she appears to have finished her meal. On the table itself there are several wine bottles. Um, there appear to be two bottles of red wine, two empty bottles of white, er, and the debris of the meal – there's a bread roll, several wine glasses. At the head of the table, um, sits a man wearing a dark jacket, striped shirt and dark tie. Er, his hair also is brushed back from his forehead. He's got sunglasses on, so it's . . . you can't see the expression in his eyes, but the expression on his face appears to be that he's very bored with the proceedings – his mouth is slightly pouted, it's turned down at the corners, he's got his eyebrows raised and you can see the wrinkles on his forehead. He's got his arms firmly folded and he doesn't really seem to be taking much interest in the proceedings, either in the food or in the conversation.

When you have finished, compare your drawing with your neighbour's drawing if you can. End of exercise 5.

Exercise 6 Listen to the following description and decide which of the fo[ur] pictures in your workbook is being described.

[*Description of second picture*]
This is a photograph of a young couple. It looks as if they're sitting at a table on the pavement outside a café, having a cup of coffee. Er, you can see the window of the café in the background of the photograph. Er, the couple are in their early twenties, I should imagine. Er, the young lady is wearing a loose-fitting, white jacket. She has blonde hair which is drawn back into a pony-tail. Er, the young man has a dark sports jacket with a white, open-necked shirt; he has short, dark hair and a moustache. Er, they both have newspapers and the youn[g] man has his newspaper open and is pointing to an article or something in the newspaper. And the young lady also has her newspaper open, but with her left hand she is pointing to the open newspaper that the young man is holding.

Have you decided? Which one was it? ....
It was the second one. Can you say why you decided it was that one? ....
Because he said the young lady was pointing at the man's newspaper with her left hand.
End of exercise 6.

Exercise 7 Describing people

Look at your workbook and answer these questions about the people in the picture. Listen to an example first:

Man: Where are they exactly?
Model: They're coming down the steps of a plane – they look as if they're returning from holiday.

Now answer the questions yourself. The model answers are for guidance only.

Man: Where are they exactly? ....
Model: They're coming down the steps of a plane.

Man: How old is the man? ....
Model: He looks as if he's in his mid-thirties.

Man: How old is the woman? ....
Model: She looks younger than him – she's thirtyish, I'd say.

Man: Has the man got a beard? ....
Model: Yes, he has a short, dark beard and a moustache.

Man: What about his hair? ....
Model: It's dark and straight. It's cut quite short and he has a parting on the left. His hair seems to be receding slightly.

Man: And his clothes? ....
Model: He's wearing a dark double-breasted blazer with a patterned shirt and a plain dark tie.

Man: What about the woman? What sort of hair has she got? ....
Model: I can't tell because she's wearing a knitted woollen hat that completely covers her hair.

Man: What's she wearing? ....
Model: She's wearing a roll-neck jumper and a loose knitted woollen coat over her shoulders. She has a medallion on a chain round her neck.

Man: Is she wearing glasses? ....
Model: Yes, she has a pair of square-shaped dark glasses on with metal rims. They could be sunglasses or normal glasses with tinted lenses.

Man: And what about her face? ....
Model: She's smiling broadly and she has a round face with a largish mouth. I can't see her eyes, because of the dark glasses.

Man: And *his* face? ....
Model: He's got a long face and his eyes are rather close together. His mouth is quite small.

Man: What sort of person do you think the woman is? ....
Model: She looks a very cheerful person, always laughing and joking.

Man: And finally what sort of person is *he*? ....
Model: He looks a rather sensitive, thoughtful man with a good sense of humour. He looks very kind. Possibly he's a bit shy.

End of exercise 7.

Exercise 8 Describing a place and people

Look at the picture in your workbook for exercise 8. This time you have to describe the people *and* where they are. Take your time to think before you start recording. If you're working alone, find a blank cassette to make your recording on. Don't use this cassette. If you're working in a language laboratory with a teacher, tell the teacher when you're ready to start and when you've finished.
End of unit 13.

There is no communication activity in this unit, but note that exercise 8 practises speaking freely. There is a key to exercise 1 in activity I, to exercise 2 in activity Q and to exercise 5 in activity Z.

Unit 14 Telling a story: narrative techniques, handling dialogue, controlling a narrative

Exercise 1 Correcting misunderstandings

In this exercise you're going to hear a story told by your friend Anne. (Anne: Hallo!) Your friend Bob (Bob: Hallo!) keeps misunderstanding the story so you will need to correct him. Look at your workbook and listen to the examples:

Anne: This is a true story about a Swiss couple, Hans and Erna W., who were in Hong Kong on holiday and went to a restaurant for a meal.
Bob: They had a meal in their hotel?
Model: No, what they did was go to a restaurant.
Anne: Anyway, they couldn't speak Chinese or even English very well, so they had to use sign language to order their meal.
Bob: They ordered their meal in German?
Model: No, what they did was use sign language.

Now listen carefully to Anne's story and correct Bob's misunderstandings. Ready?

Anne: This is a true story about a Swiss couple, Hans and Erna W., who were in Hong Kong on holiday and went to a restaurant for a meal.
Bob: They had a meal in their hotel? ....

Model: No, what they did was go to a restaurant.

Anne: Anyway, they couldn't speak Chinese or even English very well, so they had to use sign language to order their meal.

Bob: They ordered their meal in German? ....

Model: No, what they did was use sign language.

Anne: Well, this seemed to work alright. The waiter nodded and smiled and started to go to the kitchen.

Bob: The waiter shook his head and frowned? ....

Model: No, what he did was nod and smile.

Anne: Oh, and I forgot to mention they had their pet poodle, Rosa, with them and Erna reminded her husband that Rosa was hungry.

Bob: The husband had remembered the dog needed feeding? ....

Model: No, what happened was that his wife had to remind him.

Anne: Anyway, they called the waiter back and they pointed at the poodle, Rosa, and made eating gestures.

Bob: They asked the waiter to bring some food for Rosa to eat? ....

Model: Not exactly, no, what they did was point at the dog and make eating gestures.

Anne: The waiter didn't seem to understand and looked puzzled.

Bob: Oh, he understood immediately, did he? ....

Model: No, what happened was that the waiter didn't understand.

Anne: But in the end he smiled and nodded and picked up the dog and took it to the kitchen.

Bob: So he led the dog into the kitchen? ....

Model: No, what he did was carry it to the kitchen.

Anne: Hans and Erna W. were satisfied and chatted about their holiday experiences until their food was ready.

Bob: What? They sat in silence? ....

Model: No, what they did was chat about their holiday experiences.

Anne: After about an hour the waiter returned with their main course on a silver dish covered with a large silver lid.

Bob: Oh, the main course was served in a few minutes, was it? ....

Model: No, what happened was that they had to wait about an hour.

Anne: Anyway, when they lifted the silver lid they found their poodle inside, roasted and garnished with sweet and sour sauce and bamboo shoots. The couple both suffered a mild nervous collapse and took the next plane back to Zurich.

Bob: What? They ate their meal? ....

Model: No, of course not, what happened was that they both suffered a mild nervous collapse and returned to Switzerland immediately.

Bob: And that's a true story? It sounds a bit far-fetched to me.

Anne: No, it's perfectly true. Really!

End of exercise 1.

Exercise 2 Now you know the story of Hans and Erna W. and their poodle, Rosa, we'd like you to tell the story yourself. If you're working on your own you'll need to use a separate blank cassette. If you're working in a language laboratory with a teacher, tell your teacher when you're ready to begin and let your teacher know when you've finished.

Exercise 3 Look at your workbook and listen to this story. The pictures in your workbook are *lettered* but they are in the wrong order. Listen to the story and put a number beside each picture to show the correct order. If necessary, listen to the story more than once.

[*The story of Dr Crippen*]
The story of Dr Henry Horley Crippen, born in 1861, died in 1910. Dr Henry Horley Crippen was a medical doctor living in London. As a young man he met a music hall performer called Belle Elmore. They married and lived together at a little terraced house in Hilldrop Crescent in London. After they'd been married for a few years, however, the couple didn't seem to get on as well as they had done at first. Dr Crippen spent a lot more time in his surgery than he had done before. And he spent even more time after he'd employed a typist called Ethel Le Neve, because he fell in love with her. His love was returned and eventually they grew so desperate that they plotted to murder his wife. They discussed for a long time what method they should use. A gun? But no, they decided that would be too noisy. A knife? But that would be dreadfully messy. A pillow

over the face? But unfortunately Belle was a great deal larger than her husband and he felt that he wouldn't have the necessary strength to make it effective. At last they decided on poison, yes, that could be done quickly and quietly and Dr Crippen, being in the medical profession, could easily obtain some poison. This was administered to Belle, she duly died and then they had the problem of how to dispose of the body. They tried to burn it out in the garden, but this was not successful, and eventually they buried it in the cellar of their house. All was well for a time, but unfortunately they heard that the police had some clues and that they were hunting for the couple to ask them some questions. They both took fright and they decided to escape to America. Ethel disguised herself as a young boy – she was a very slim girl – and they escaped together on a ship bound for America. But they spent so much time together on board the ship that the captain became suspicious in the end and he radioed the police in England. Inspector Dew, who was in charge of the case, boarded a faster ship which was on its way to Canada, overtook their ship and boarded it. They were both arrested on board the ship, brought back to London, the trial took place and they were both condemned to death and they were hanged in 1910. This was the first time that an arrest of this kind had been made through ship-to-shore radio.

Listen to the story again if you have any doubts as to the correct order. ....
The correct answers are next on this tape.
This is the correct order: Picture C is the first one, E the second, G the third, D is fourth, H is fifth, B is sixth, F is seventh and A is eighth.

Now that you know the story, try telling it in your own words. If you're working alone, use a blank cassette for your recording. If you're working in a language laboratory, tell your teacher when you're ready to start and when you've finished.

Exercise 4 Look at your workbook and listen to this model version of the cartoon strip there. Later you will have to tell the same story in your own words.

[*The story of Mr Jones, the smuggler*]
This story concerns a fellow – well, let's call him Mr Jones – who'd been on holiday in North America. He'd had a good time, spent a lot of money, and then on the very last day of his

holiday he was walking down the street when his attention was caught by something in the window of a shop selling photographic equipment. There was a single-lens reflex camera for the price of $299. He went into the shop, examined it, gave it a good looking-over and thought to himself well this is a real bargain, this is very cheap. However, he'd spent nearly all the money he'd taken with him on holiday. He only had a few traveller's cheques left, but because it was a bargain, he paid them and took his camera home. Well, he was still feeling quite pleased with himself until he got onto the plane. Sitting there, he began to feel a little nervous, because it came into his mind the prospect of trying to get the camera through customs. He imagined being stopped by a customs officer . . . Well, he didn't have any more money with him, he thought he might land himself in trouble. He could see the customs man opening the bag, finding the camera – there was no point in trying to hide it under his clothes. By the time he reached his destination and came through the customs he was feeling pretty terrified. But he put a bold front on it, put a big smile on his face, walked through the green channel and luckily enough he got through without being stopped.

Now it's your turn to tell the story. Imagine you are the hero of the story and tell it as if it really happened to you. If you're working alone, use a blank cassette. If you're working in a language laboratory, let your teacher know when you're ready to start and when you've finished.
There is a communication activity next, for which you need to find a partner, the instructions are printed in your workbook.
End of unit 14.

In the communication activity one student looks at activity E, while the other looks at activity R. Each has half of the pictures from a strip cartoon. Each student has to tell the parts of the story he or she knows from the pictures in the activity.
Note that there are free-speaking practice activities in exercises 2, 3 and 4.

Unit 15 Dealing with moods and feelings: anger, sadness, indifference. Saying goodbye

Exercise 1 Reacting to someone who's angry

In this exercise you're going to hear different people who are angry about different things. Try to calm them down. Imagine they are all friends. Here are two examples to help you:

Friend 1: Oh no! I've spilt coffee all over my dress – it's ruined!
Model: Oh dear, that *is* bad. But there's no need to get so upset, if you soak it in cold water it'll come out.

Friend 2: Thirty-five minutes I had to wait! And when the bus finally came I had to stand up all the way!
Model: Take it easy! It's alright now, sit down and have a rest.

Now be sympathetic and try to calm your friends. The model answers are for guidance only. Ready?

Friend 1: Oh no! Look, I've just spilt coffee all over my dress – it's ruined! ....
Model: There's no need to get so upset. If you soak it in cold water the stain will probably come out.

Friend 2: Thirty-five minutes I had to wait! And when the bus did come at last I had to stand up all the way here!
....
Model: Take it easy! Have a seat, sit down and relax!

Friend 1: I've just about had enough of my boss! He's making my life impossible. How the hell can I work for a man like that? ....
Model: Oh, I'm sure it's not as bad as all that. Why don't you talk to him and explain what the problem is?

Friend 2: That's absolutely marvellous! I've left all my books on the bus! ....
Model: There's no need to get so upset. You can go to the lost property office and see if they've been handed in.

Friend 1: So there I was – 7.30 at the airport! I had to get up at 6, do you realize that! Nobody told *me* the planes were on strike! ....
Model: I'm sorry to hear that. If I'd known I'd have told you.

Friend 2: Where the hell's my comb? I suppose you borrowed it again and you've forgotten where you put it! It's *my* comb! ....

Model: Oh, I'm ever so sorry. I think it's in my pocket. Yes here you are. Sorry!

Friend 1: I've just heard my boss is on holiday for three weeks and I've got to fill in for him! He never told *me* and I don't know what's supposed to be done. Typical! ....

Model: Don't you think you're overreacting a bit? I mean, I'm sure he's taken care of everything. He's probably left you some notes.

Friend 2: Look here! Do you realize what time it is? You said you'd meet me half an hour ago outside! What on earth have you been doing? ....

Model: Oh, goodness! Yes, look, I'm terribly sorry, but I've been so busy with these exercises that it completely slipped my mind. Sorry!

End of exercise 1.

Exercise 2 Cheering up a sad friend

In this exercise your friends are all unhappy. We'd like *you* to try to cheer them up a bit. Here are two examples:

Friend 1: I feel awful! I've got this terrible headache.

Model: Oh, what a shame! Look, I've got some aspirins – take a couple of these.

Friend 2: I just don't know what to do! My car's got to be repaired and it's sure to cost the earth.

Model: Come on! It can't be as bad as all that. You could get it fixed next month when you've got some more money.

Now try to cheer your friends up yourself. Ready?

Friend 1: Ohh, I feel terrible! I've got another one of my headaches. ....

Model: Oh, what a shame! Take a couple of these aspirins and you'll soon feel better.

Friend 2: What am I going to do? It's going to cost the earth to have my car fixed and I've got to have it done. ....

Model: Come on! It can't be as bad as all that. Why don't you get it fixed next month when you've got a bit more money?

Friend 1: Oh dear! The doctor says I've got to eat less. I *can't* stop eating sweets and cakes. I'll go mad, I know I will! ....
Model: Cheer up! It'll be OK. You'll soon get used to it!

Friend 2: I just don't know what to do! My boss says if my work doesn't improve I'll get the sack! ....
Model: Don't worry about it! Just work a bit harder, be nice to him and it'll be alright, I'm sure it will.

Friend 1: I can't take any more! He's leaving me! He's found someone else! What am I going to do? ....
Model: Try and look on the bright side – it's probably all for the best. You'll find someone else soon enough.

Friend 2: It's a disaster! I've left all the notes I've made in my English lessons on the train. I'll never get them back! All my studies wasted! ....
Model: Cheer up! You can borrow my notes and copy them out – it might even help you to remember everything better.

Friend 1: That's it! It's the end! I've spent all my money and I won't be able to eat again till next month. I'll probably starve to death! ....
Model: Come on! It's not as bad as all that. I'll lend you some money. How much do you need?

Friend 2: Well, this is it! I'm off. I don't suppose we'll ever see each other again. I'm really going to miss you. ....
Model: I'm going to miss you, too. Hey look, why don't we have a drink together before you go?

End of exercise 2.

Exercise 3 Trying to interest someone

In this exercise you'll hear various people who are very *un*enthusiastic about some plans. Try to interest them by pointing out the advantages. Here are two examples, notice the intonation:

Friend 1: I don't want to go to the cinema. I've heard it's a very bad film.
Model: Oh, I don't think it's all that bad – in fact, I think you'll find it's very good.

Friend 2: Hmm, I don't think it's a good idea to go by train. Trains are always terribly slow.
Model: Oh, I don't think they're all that slow – in fact, I think you'll find they're very fast.

Now, follow the pattern and point out how your friends' impressions are mistaken. Be careful about your intonation.

Friend 1: No, I don't feel like going to the cinema. I've heard that film's awfully bad, anyway. ....
Model: Oh, I don't think it's all that bad – in fact, I think you'll find it's very good.

Friend 2: There's no point in going by train. Trains are always terribly slow. ....
Model: Oh, I don't think they're all that slow – in fact, I think you'll find they're very fast.

Friend 1: What's the point of reading that book? It looks ever so boring. ....
Model: Oh, I don't think it's all that boring – in fact, I thin you'll find it's very interesting.

Friend 2: It looks to me as if that room will be very noisy – I mean it's at the front of the house. ....
Model: Oh, I don't think it's all that noisy – in fact, I think you'll find it's very quiet.

Friend 1: I don't really want to meet your friend. He looks a bit stupid to me. ....
Model: Oh, I don't think he's all that stupid – in fact, I thin you'll find he's very intelligent.

Friend 2: I suppose it's a good idea to go away for the weeken The trouble is it's sure to be tiring. ....
Model: Oh, I don't think it'll be all that tiring – in fact, I think you'll find it's very relaxing.

Friend 1: I'm not going to do any more English lessons. They'(be absolutely useless to me. ....
Model: Oh, I don't think they'd be useless at all – in fact, I'm sure you'd find them very worthwhile.
Friend 1: Really? ....
Model: Yes, definitely!

End of exercise 3.

Exercise 4 Reacting to the unexpected

In this exercise you're going to hear various people saying different things to you. Remembering all the exercises we've done in this course, try to react appropriately to each person. Here are two examples first:

Old lady: Oh dear, I've dropped my purse!
Model: Oh, let me pick it up for you. Here you are!

Middle-aged man: Lovely weather for the time of year, isn't it?
Model: Mmm yes, it certainly it. Let's hope it lasts for the weekend.

Now it's your turn. The model answers are for guidance only in this exercise.

Old lady: Oh dear, oh dear! I've dropped my purse on the floor. ....
Model: Oh, let me pick it up for you. Here you are!

Middle-aged man: Terrible weather today, isn't it? ....
Model: Oh yes, it's dreadful, isn't it. Still, let's hope it gets better before the weekend!

Young man: I'm going out to a disco tonight. Like to come along? ....
Model: Oh, that'd be nice, but I'm afraid I'm a bit tied up tonight. Perhaps some other time, though.

Upper-class lady: Oh I say, I'm terribly sorry. Was that your foot? ....
Model: I'm afraid so, but don't worry, it didn't hurt very much and I've got another one.

Little girl: My ball's gone over the fence and I'm afraid to go and ask for it back. ....
Model: Well, you'll just have to, I'm afraid. Ring the bell and tell the lady you're very sorry.

Foreigner: Yes, I come from China – from Shanghai in fact. ....
Model: Oh really, that's interesting. I've always wanted to go there. What's it like there?

Young woman: Hallo. You look ever so tired. Didn't you get much sleep last night? ....

Model:	Well, I went to bed at the usual time, but f some reason I woke up terribly early and I didn't manage to get back to sleep.
Young woman:	What would you do if you found £5 in the street? ....
Model:	Difficult to say, but I suppose I'd take it to the police station. On the other hand I mig decide to pocket it – if there was no-one looking!
Old lady:	Excuse me, could you tell me the way to th town centre? ....
Model:	I'm not quite sure actually, you see I'm a stranger here myself. Sorry!

End of exercise 4.

Exercise 5 Reacting to the unexpected

In this exercise you're going to hear some more people speakin to you. React in the most appropriate way you can. There are no model answers, but here's one example to help you:

Young man:	I really enjoy Western films, don't you?
Model:	Well no, not really, I find them all a bit predictable. And I can't stand the way th Indians always get killed.

Now it's your turn. There are no model answers. Ready?

Young man:	I think James Bond films are great, don't you? ....
Middle-aged woman:	Would you mind not smoking in here. It's a no-smoking area you know. ....
Young man:	Hallo! Nice to see you again! What've you been doing with yourself since I last saw you? ....
Old man:	Do you happen to have the time on you, by any chance? ....
Old man:	Oh, well, do you know if the bus to town has left yet? ....
Woman:	Tapes sometimes break, don't they. What if this tape you're using broke, what would you do? ....

Scotsman:	Yes, I come from Auchterhellweet in Perthshire. ....
Woman:	Where did he say he came from? ....
Man:	What do you think of these exercises you've been doing? ....
Man:	Really? Are you being honest? ....
Woman:	Why don't you turn off this tape, go outside and get some fresh air? ....
Man:	Well, this is the end nearly, I'd better say goodbye. It's been nice talking to you. ....
Woman:	See you! ....
Child:	Byebye! ....
Man:	Bye for now! ....
Woman:	Thanks for everything! ....
Man:	Don't forget to drop me a line! ....
Woman:	I'm going to miss you, you know! ....
Man:	Goodbye to you and the very best of luck! ....

And that really is the end of this exercise and the end of the last unit of these recorded exercises.
All: Bye! ....

There is no communication activity in this unit, but you might like to ask your students to speak freely for one minute on 'What you think of these exercises'.